SHORT FILMS 2.0

GETTING NOTICED IN THE YOUTUBE AGE

BY

MIKEL J. WISLER

www.mikelwisler.com/shortfilms20

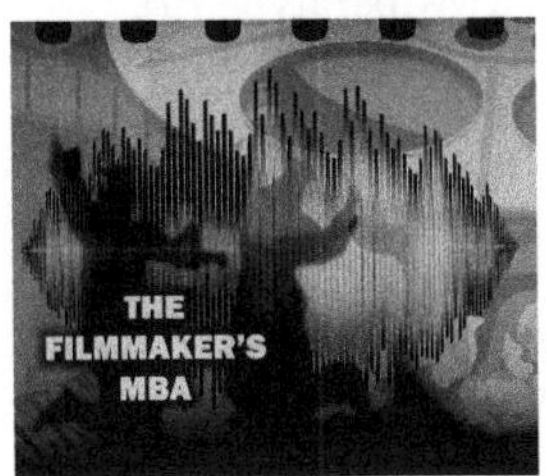

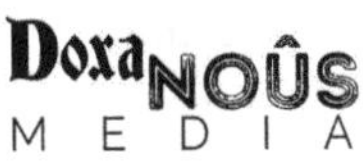

Short Films 2.0: Getting Noticed in the YouTube Age

Published by The Filmmaker's MBA, an imprint of DoxaNous Media, LLC
803 N. Western Avenue
Marion, Indiana 46952
www.doxanousmedia.com

Copy Editors: Béckie Rankin, Eric Bumpus
Cover Photography and Graphic Design: Mikel J. Wisler

Printed in the United States of America

ISBN-13: 978-1-7325307-0-6 (pbk)
ISBN-13: 978-1-952375-09-5 (ebk)

Type Face: the text of this book is printed using PT Serif.
Copyright © 2009 ParaType Ltd (http://www.paratype.ru).
PT Serif is licensed under the Paratype PT Sans Free Font License v1.00.

Cover and chapter title font: Bebas, Flat-it License v1.00, freeware typeface (http://flat-it.com).

Screenplays: Courier Prime, Copyright © 2013, Quote-Unquote Apps (http://quoteunquoteapps.com), with Reserved Font Name Courier Prime. SIL Open Font License v1.10.

For information about the author, visit: www.mikelwisler.com

First Digital Edition: May 2016
First Print Edition: June 2016
23 24 25 26 27 28 | 10 9 8 7 6 5

Praise for Mikel J. Wisler's Short Films:

“Parallel” is a beautiful cinematic tone poem that fiercely champions the idea of everlasting love. It’s a stunning achievement in romantic sci-fi.

- Philip Smolen's review of "Parallel"
Rogue Cinema

“Parallel” has a feature film’s worth of story it tells in 11 minutes. That may make it sound convoluted, but it’s a very clear-eyed story, with emotional journeys experienced that would normally take two hours, but here are followed, easily and un-rushed, in minutes. ... it’s quite an experience on not just it’s main character, but the viewer, as well.

- Brian Skutle's review of "Parallel"
Sonic-Cinema.com

Wisler and company deliver a thinking person's short film that taps into some pretty primitive areas, including what it means to exist in the field of time, what it means to live, to love and lose and finally to die. It's serious, it's smart, it’s even a bit of a tear jerker.

- Nicholas La Salla's review of "Parallel"
Forest City Short Film Review

[Playing with Ice] is a wonderful and satisfying short that speaks volumes about what we hold inside and the damage it causes. Wisler has made a life-affirming and nifty pseudo sci-fi movie all at the same time. Bravo!

- Philip Smolen's review of "Playing with Ice"
Rogue Cinema

... the execution is flawless... do yourself a favor, watch the thing twice, back to back—only the second time will show how spot-on the performances really are!

- Mike Haberfelner’s review of “Intrigue”
[(re)Search my Trash]

Also written by Mikel J. Wisler

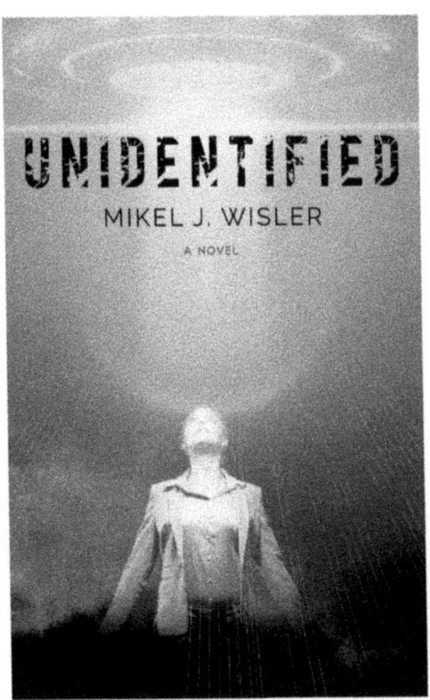

One year ago, a boy mysteriously went missing after claiming to have been abducted by extraterrestrial beings multiple times. No trace of him has ever been found.

Now, Boston-based Special Agent for the FBI, Nicole Mitchell, is brought back from administrative leave when a girl in the same New Hampshire town also claims to have been abducted. The girl's story bears eerie similarities to the case of the missing boy Mitchell investigated the year before.

Certain that someone is using the powerful suggestion of UFOs and the alien abduction scenario to kidnap these kids, Mitchell enlists the help of paranormal debunking psychiatrist, Dr. Alan Evans. But, who among the locals knows the truth? Is it the girl's parents? The peculiar new pastor in town? The local police? As the case unfolds, Mitchell and Evans are confronted with a much darker and far more sinister reality than they ever expected. Nothing could have prepared them for what they are about to encounter.

"Unidentified is full of spookiness and reversals and surprises and fun. I can't wait for the movie."

- Dave Schmelzer (Editor-in-chief: hellohoratio.com)

FOR ANDREW GILBERT

CONTENTS

APPENDICES

ACKNOWLEDGEMENTS

I have been making short films for years and as a result there are so many people that should be thanked for their help and influence in my development as a filmmaker and storyteller. Every cast and crew I've worked with has taught me so much! Thank you to all of these people, though I dare not name everyone here as the list would be a book all its own.

Thank you to my wife, Danae, who has supported my crazy endeavors for a very long time! I must thank my early short filmmaking partners: Andrew Gilbert, Scott Peercy, Jeremiah Hawn, Ben Bowers, Chris Evans, and Andrew Shaw with whom I made so many fun and early projects along with a lot of mistakes and missteps that taught me so much. Thank you to the Los Angeles Film Studies Center for the invaluable lessons and hands-on experience.

Thank you to Stories by the River and Kristina and Dominic Stone Kaiser for engaging directly in the act of making short films and seeing their value as a medium for exploring life's meaning. My many thanks to Trevor Duke, who gave feedback on an early draft of this manuscript, and for being a fantastic partner in short filmmaking. Thanks to Eric Bumpus for his continued encouragement and enthusiasm for this particular book as well as my short films and for helping significantly with the editing process. Thank you to Béckie Rankin for the insightful editing and feedback on this manuscript and for furthering the dialogue about short filmmaking by inviting me to speak to her high school students.

I must specifically thank Randy Zella Varaguas. This whole book first started out as a very simple outline for a short talk she asked me to give at an event she organized at the Hull Film Office. After giving that talk, I got to thinking that the information I covered might be of value to a lot more people than I initially thought.

Finally, even though he's no longer with us, I sincerely must thank my grandpa, Bob Wisler, for allowing the very young and energetic kid I was so many years ago to constantly borrow his video camera and run off into the woods or down the road or into the creek to try my hand at creating something resembling motion pictures. In the process I took my first early and shaky steps in visual storytelling.

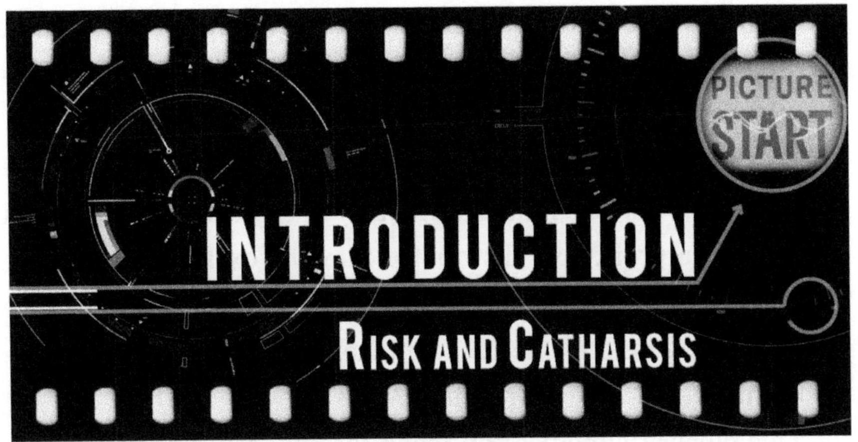

We live in an extremely fast-paced and media-saturated world. So, how can new and aspiring filmmakers stand out? Over the last decade of making short films, I have asked myself this question often. It has been an amazing time to make shorts for many reasons. In particular, my work making short films coincided with the first ten years of YouTube, which has proven to be a unique period of time for new filmmakers. The world of short filmmaking and distribution has been under rapid change for several years. Trying to make sense of all these changes and how to take advantage of new opportunities can be challenging. In preparing to give a talk a while back at the Hull Film Office about making short films, I outlined what I felt has happened in recent years to the medium and how new filmmakers can make the most of these changes. As I looked around at various books after the presentation, I realized that there seems to be little material covering the recent evolution of short films in a comprehensive way. So, if you're ready to dive into making a short film in this new age of online media, grab a coffee and let's get busy exploring how you can set yourself up for success by embracing change and dispelling some outdated ideas!

Before we get into the nitty-gritty details, though, I think it might be helpful to stop and ask a bigger question first: Why make short films?

In the world of movies, feature-length films dominate the cultural focus and the financial viability of creating a film that can be sold for a profit to a distributor remains exclusive to feature films. As I write this, I am in development for my first feature film, but long before I decided to take on a feature film, I made and continue to make short films. Why?

One clear argument often made for why aspiring filmmakers should value starting off their career by making short films is that they will learn through experience and become far more prepared for the task of making a feature film. This is quite true. In the words of Michael Rabiger, "short films still require their makers to conquer the full range of production, authorship, and stylistic problems—but in a small compass and small cost."[1] I've seen—even worked with—filmmakers whose first feature films faced many challenges due to the inexperience of the director. I am convinced that many such issues could have been avoided had they taken the time to make a few short films first.

However, there is so much more to short films than just learning the filmmaking craft! For a while I felt I was done with short films and that my time would be better spent focusing exclusively on how to get a feature film funded. One major development in my life changed all of that.

The following story is probably rather odd-sounding, but please hear me out. In 2010, I got involved with a small and unconventional start-up church. I know. It's true. I'm one of

---

[1] *Directing: Film Techniques and Aesthetics* by Michael Rabiger, 1997, Focal Press. Page 6.

those goofballs that actually goes to church (and rather likes it, no less). But you see, this church is not quite like any other place I've been. The River Church, in Quincy, Massachusetts, is a rather unique place. There, for the first time in my life, rather than feeling like my passion for the arts pitted me against my faith community, I find it to be embraced and sought out. For example, I began running The River Film Forum, a monthly event designed around watching movies with people from all walks of life and engaging in meaningful conversations about what such stories have to offer us in terms of examining life. Here is a community of people genuinely interested in hearing diverse stories and various perspectives as each of us journeys through life together.

In fact, movies became such an important part of what we do as a faith community, that even as part of our Sunday morning worship service we started occasionally using short films as the central piece of the day's talk. By focusing on the shared experience of a brief story, we discovered something unique and amazing: short films can allow us to dive right into some of the deepest and darkest areas of the human heart and mind in a matter of minutes. And the conversations that ensue are unlike any other conversations I've encountered in my life-long journey of faith!

So when Kristina Stone Kaiser, my pastor, asked me if we could possibly make short films that offered both opportunities for local filmmakers to gain experience and give us stories that could spark meaningful conversations, it was the start of an exciting new adventure. In 2012, we created Stories by the River (SbtR).[2] Now I know what you're probably thinking. It's probably something along the lines of, "Oh God, no! A church making short

---

[2] See www.StoriesByTheRiver.org for more information.

films! Ugh!" Let me put your mind at ease by expressing with all honesty that I am pretty sure no one in the world hates the agenda-driven drivel that is the majority of faith-based movies more than me.[3] Making "those kinds" of films is not at all our objective! In fact, many of the people we work with in making short films come from diverse perspectives and backgrounds. And, rather than push a specific agenda, we prefer to present stories and ask questions about life. After all, propaganda seeks only to push an agenda, but good art is less didactic, and genuinely wrestles with life. We are interested in the latter.

When done well, short films offer us an opportunity to explore life together with ample time for conversation. A short film that might only last ten or twenty or thirty minutes is a brief moment where you and I can share the experience of a story that offers us common ground for real conversations about things we might not otherwise normally talk about. And, what I love about short films specifically is that, unlike a feature film, there's no room for distractions. We have to dive quickly into the characters and expose the central problem they are facing in this moment. There's a fine art to a well-crafted short film as we seek to draw in the audience and give them just enough information so the story naturally slips forward with a sense of inevitability. Good short film scripts are lean and focused!

As a filmmaker, I can also take risks with short films, which I might never have been able to with a feature film due to the many financial concerns involved with making a feature. The first film I directed for Stories by the River was "A Silent Universe",[4] a non-

---

[3] I apologize to those who feel excited about overtly Christian movies that are, in my opinion, strong on message and short on everything else. I believe that we can do far better!

[4] Produced in 2012, available at www.StoriesByTheRiver.org.

traditional science fiction film that uses the scenario of an alien invasion as a means to trap our two characters, brothers at odds, in an old garage and force them to navigate some of life's toughest questions (which even I'd rather avoid on most days, if I'm being honest). In the face of what seems to be the complete absence of hope, can these two brothers find a reason to go on? Is doubt and despair the only appropriate response when confronted with an ugly and violent world?

In 2013, I took a personal risk with a short film I directed for Stories by the River. I chose to tell a story that is quite important to me, but also stands well outside the perspectives of many people I dearly love, even as we disagree on this important issue. The short film "Playing with Ice" tells the story of a gay young woman who interviews to become part of an aggressive scientific experiment because she feels rejected and alone after being cast off by her family due to her sexual orientation. For twenty minutes we get to dive into Jocelyn's pain at being deeply wounded. What's more, we learn that she's not the only one who has been profoundly hurt by fear and misguided ideas. Emma, the woman interviewing Jocelyn, drops her guard and reveals her own painful story. Is avoidance or denial the answer for these characters in light of the unfair and unloving treatment they have been given? Or, can they find acceptance and love right here and now? The film is brief: a high-pressure situation and an amazingly challenging story to tell. It really stretched me as a filmmaker. It's also one of the stories I'm most proud of being able to help bring to life. It has gone on to play at several festivals, including one of the top LGBT festivals in France.

By helping to launch and run Stories by the River, I have learned that short films need not serve exclusively as proof I know filmmaking technique well enough to be trusted to make a functional feature film. I do hope my experience in making short films will help instill confidence in my eventual partners in making feature films, but what if I never get the opportunity to make a feature film? Have I wasted my time making short films? I don't think so! If there's one thing that I really want to get across, it is that when I set out to tell a story—short, feature, or novel—it comes from that central and secret place deep inside my heart that desperately cries out for meaning and love, for understanding and connection. Now, this doesn't mean I only make serious movies, as I find comedy often provides great insight into some of our deepest hurts and biggest longings. In fact, one of my most recent films is a very short comedy I wrote and directed for Stories by the River called "Intrigue."[5]

So, why do I make short films? I make short films because they allow me to wrestle with life! They allow me the freedom to take risks that I might otherwise never be able to take on larger projects. These risks help me grow as an artist and can be personally quite fulfilling. Short films force me to be a better storyteller. There is no room for digressions and distractions. Often times, I have to know the characters I'm creating in just as great a depth as the ones I've created for various feature film scripts I've written. Why? Because I'm only giving you a tiny glimpse of these characters. But, in these precious few minutes during which you have hopefully given my humble film your attention, I hope you sense in these characters (and in the storyteller behind them) kindred spirits in this journey through life as we all, in our own way, seek to understand and be understood; as we all are lonely, but hopefully not alone.

---

[5] Produced in 2015, available at www.StoriesByTheRiver.org.

These are stories that sometimes form slowly and other times they spring into my mind nearly fully formed, as was the case with my 2015 Stories by the River short film, "Parallel."[6] And, over the course of time—through each draft; through conversations with my cinematographer and producers; through rehearsals with the cast; through the shooting and editing process—they prove themselves to be stories that demand to be told. As a filmmaker, I simply hope to get out of the way and allow it to happen, releasing these stories into the great unknown of our digital age in hopes that even if I never hear about it, someone somewhere out there has a moment of profound and real catharsis that inspires them—even in some small way—to look at life with new eyes, with a fresh perspective.

That is why I continue to make and love short films. I have dedicated a large amount of my time to understanding how short films work and how they differ from feature films. In fact, I was recently asked to be part of the judging panel for Digi60 Filmmakers' Festival, which focuses on challenging filmmakers to tell a story in two-and-a-half-minutes. The more I learn about how short films are changing today, the more I believe in sharing such information from my years of studying and making short films. That is why I have chosen to write this book: as a means to help other filmmakers explore the amazing and ever evolving medium of short films. One thing has become abundantly clear to me: the very nature of short films has dramatically and fundamentally changed over the last decade. With my experiences as a filmmaker, as a producer and distributor with Stories by the River, and as a festival judge for SbtR and Digi60, I have come to understand that much is changing quickly in terms of how short

---

[6] Available at www.StoriesByTheRiver.org.

films are made, how short they are, what they accomplish, and how they reach their intended audience. Innovations and changes to the medium will continue in the coming decades. With this in mind, my goal with this book is to launch a helpful dialogue about the evolution of short films that will equip new filmmakers with vital knowledge to dive into this exciting medium with confidence.[7]

---

[7] Most of this introduction first appeared as a blog entry I was invited to guest write for www.iloveshortfilms.com in 2014.

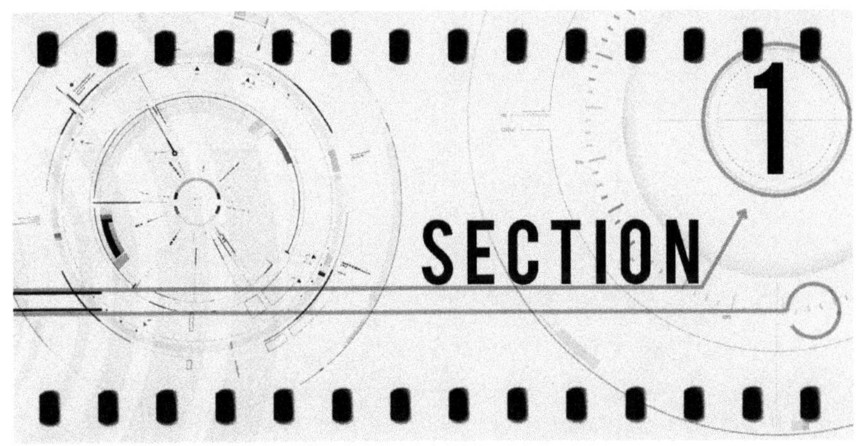

Understanding Short Films in the Digital Age

What they were, what they are, and what they are becoming.

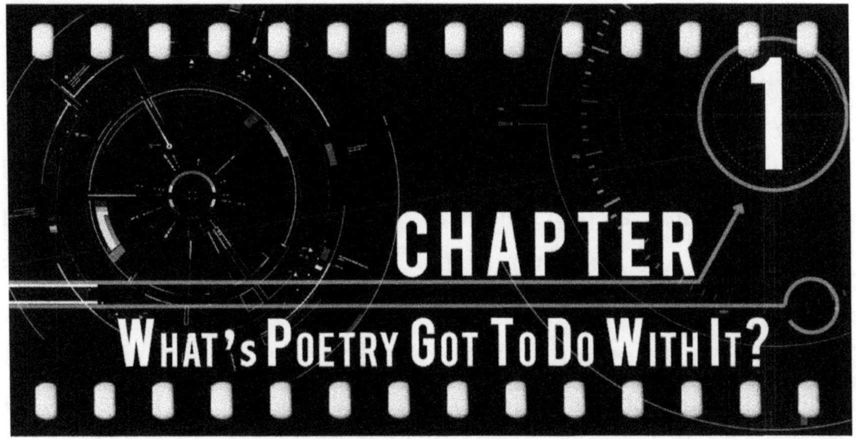

Chapter 1: What's Poetry Got To Do With It?

When I first started out as a filmmaker, I thought of short films as a means to prove I had what it takes to make feature films. To some degree, this is a good reason to get started with shorts. In fact, this may well be your reason. There's nothing wrong with using shorts as a starting ground: to prove you have the skills to make feature films. However, the process to prove those skills is not quite the same as when I started out. I want to share a little of my story with you so you can see how I've come to my current perspective on short films. Hopefully, you can then learn from my mistakes and be better equipped to dive into the current short film market with something that stands out.

While attending the Los Angeles Film Studies Center (LAFSC) during the spring of 2003, I had to make several projects that ranged from thirty seconds to three minutes. All of these projects where silent films. We had the option to shoot either on MiniDV or on Super8 film. I opted to shoot everything on Super8 as I knew the limited running time of the film stock would force me to plan thoroughly. I also knew that this was likely the only time in my life I would have the opportunity to shoot on film, and thus learn to deal with the unique challenges of lighting and properly exposing celluloid.[8]

Later, while I was still in college, I made a short film that ran thirty-six minutes. Following college, I made two short films: my first films in HD. The second of those films was a short called "Cellar Door," a psychological thriller that ran thirty-seven minutes. It was the first of my early films that made it into festivals and even won a small completion grant.[9] Following that, I made a thirty-minute psychological thriller. It got into several festivals and won an award at a notable festival in Philadelphia for its screenplay.[10] These early short films were truly miniature feature films. They had distinct three act structures as one might expect to see in a two-hour movie.

I continued making short films with this concept in mind. But, I also continued to cut back on the length of scripts. After all, it took five long consecutive days to shoot "Cellar Door" and two long weekends to shoot "Cold October." Andrew Gilbert, my fellow writer and producer, and I were making these shorts with incredibly limited resources that we managed to cobble together ourselves. One thing became clear: shooting needed to be quicker! We could not sustain the cost in money and time required to shoot such long short films. Thus began my personal development in seeing the great value of brevity in short films.

---

[8] So far, that has remained the case. I have yet to shoot more projects on celluloid. And, with the advancement of digital technology, it seems less likely I will in the future.

[9] "Cellar Door" was awarded the 2007 Cinephile Film Arts Grant, in Bloomington, Indiana.

[10] "Cold October," co-written by Andrew Gilbert & Mikel J. Wisler, directed by Wisler, winner of Best Screenplay at the 2009 Terror Film Festival in Philadelphia, Pennsylvania.

Brevity, Focus, and Discipline

Looking at short films today, it is clear to me that shorts require an even greater amount of focus and discipline upon the part of the storytellers making them.[11] While a feature film can get away with a weak moment, or a scene that maybe drags just a little, or an awkward bit of cutting or dialogue that is forgotten an hour later when the credits roll, a short film does not have this luxury; audiences poise themselves differently for a shorter film and are able to take in and remember so much more. In a very real sense, the filmmaking in short films is far more naked and visible than in feature films. A tiny flaw in a short film represents such a significant portion of the whole project.

In other words, short films are at a disadvantage as a filmmaker's skills are quite exposed. This is both an intimidating and exhilarating aspect of short filmmaking. As a filmmaker, you are quite vulnerable, but you are also ideally poised to learn from mistakes. Where a feature film audience might not dive into the nitty-gritty of what really worked and didn't work about the pacing of the editing, shot choice, camera movement, or dialogue writing, a short film's brevity does not allow the audience to slip into its usual movie-watching mode.[12] The result of this difference is that audiences are more sensitive to the mechanics of filmmaking. On the one hand, this can be daunting to new filmmakers (though most are naive enough to not worry about this, and that's a good and necessary thing), but on the other hand, this nakedness of the short filmmaking process allows for

---

[11] In Chapter Two, I explore how this evolution happened and why brevity has become the key to effective short filmmaking.

[12] In Chapter Three, I address how short films are experienced and why this further exposes short films to critical scrutiny.

greater growth in new filmmakers willing to endure critical feedback on early projects. This is definitely how I learned!

Another factor that separates feature films and shorts is the need in longer films for subplots. With most feature films, there are multiple characters that are often experiencing their own journeys of discovery and transformation, and thus they get some attention, and their storylines have to be addressed and resolved as they intersect with the main story. Subplots make for a strong feature film, but they generally take away from short films. By and large, they just slow a short film down and cause the movie to overstay its welcome. The good news is when writing a short film script there is no need to develop subplots. The challenge, however, is that good short films must remain impeccably focused. Linda J. Cowgill draws the following comparison from another form of storytelling, "Just as the short story writer envies the novelist's freedom to leisurely establish mood and story, the short film writer has a difficult job in structuring his story so that the characters, theme and plot all prove satisfying in a shorter framework."[13]

This is what I mean when I say that short films require a greater level of focus and discipline. As storytellers seeking to make a short film, you and I do not have the luxuries of greater time and space that often accompany feature films (or novels). Not to mention, most short films are made with minimal or no budget at all, a limitation that adds challenges and possibilities.[14] This does not mean that there isn't a great level of focus and discipline required when making an effective feature film. I assure

---

[13] *Writing Short Films* by Linda J. Cowgill, Watson-Guptill Publications, 2005. Page xiv.

[14] In Chapter Four, I discuss how to embrace making short films on a limited budget.

you there is, but the constraints on a short film impose unique requirements on filmmakers, especially today!

I was once hired to be the final polishing editor on a feature film. It was a good film, but it lagged at points. It was not the best version of the story when I came aboard. By the end of the process, through conversations with the director and producer and a lot of loving and painstaking work, we had cut out nearly thirty minutes of the film. In fact, I'd completely deleted a character from the story. As it turned out, we came to recognize that this particular character added nothing to the progression of the plot or the central conflict of the story. The information we learned in scenes between this supporting character and the main character either was repeated elsewhere or did not have a profound enough impact on the story to be missed when it was simply taken away. The end result of this editing process was that we arrived at a much stronger version of the film that moved with purpose and momentum. In other words, we crafted a far more watchable movie.

The other end result of this experience was that it taught me so much as a writer about what does and doesn't work once you get to the editing room. This is true whether I am working on a feature or short screenplay. I had read the script for the above feature before the film had gone into production. I served as the film's assistant director, so I was intimately acquainted with every moment of production. I liked the script, but I was also younger and not quite as experienced in those days. Seeing first hand just how much could be—in fact, needed to be—cut out of the film to make it an engaging experience for audiences has forever changed how I read scripts today. It has also fundamentally changed how I write scripts!

So, yes, great discipline is required when writing a feature film script, but allow me to propose a theory. I believe, as far as literary forms of storytelling, feature films have more in common with short stories than they do with novels. Novels take hours to read, can often include several main characters, can span large amounts of time and space, and can ultimately be quite a cerebral experience. Short stories, on the other hand, tend to focus on fewer characters, on singular events, and often drop us right into the middle of an emotive experience. Because of these things, I often find that films adapted from short stories tend to flow better than films adapted from novels. In the case of Phillip K. Dick's short story, "Minority Report," the film version actually expands on some of the ideas in the original short story. Meanwhile, whole characters have to be excluded from adaptations of many novels.[15]

I bring all of this up to make this point: If feature films are more like short stories in nature, that must mean most short films are in fact closer to flash fiction, or possibly poetry. Consider these words from filmmaker and writer Michael Rabiger:

> Regrettably the short film subject is often considered beneath the director with serious intentions. This is like would-be novelists rejecting poetry and the short story as unworthy mediums. The short film is actually closest to the poetic form, for it requires deft characterization, a compressed narrative style, and something to say that is focused and fresh in voice. A good five- to ten-minute film

---

[15] Tom Bombadil is excluded from *The Lord of the Rings* trilogy of films, which ultimately makes the most sense given the nature and scope of the movies compared to the books and their connection to the broader world and story that J.R.R. Tolkien was creating, in which Bombadil is a vital presence.

> is actually more demanding to make than a passable thirty minute one.[16]

Rabiger makes no bones about it. Making a good short film is hard work. In fact, I might go as far as to suggest it's likely harder to make a good short film than it is to make a good feature film, which can be a pretty deflating thought, but hang in there. I think back on my own start in short films and it's no wonder I started out making films that came in well over thirty minutes in length. As Rabiger points out, it was just plain easier to write films that long. I had not yet developed enough discipline as a storyteller to pull off something shorter. Go figure. Yet somehow, new filmmakers are expected to start with short films instead of features. Obviously it is generally much cheaper to shoot a short film than a feature, but I would also suggest that precisely because of the greater level of difficulty in mastering effective storytelling within short films that new filmmakers must take on short films before embarking on feature films with all their inherent financial pressures.

So, what's a new filmmaker hoping to make a good short film to do?

Go Shorter

The name of the game is brevity! There is really no room for extraneous information and there is no time for lengthy exposition and mood setting. We must simply dive in. As Cowgill points out in her book *Writing Short Films*, "In a short film,

---

[16] *Directing: Film Techniques and Aesthetics* by Michael Rabiger, Focal Press, 1997. Page 211.

gratuitous information is especially problematic; it will delay action and obscure information that is truly important."[17]

It seems to me that there are two ways one can approach brevity: as a burdensome limitation or the very fuel for your creativity. Most feature films require multiple characters and numerous locations. Few features can effectively pull off single location stories. Even horror movies that might take place entirely in one haunted house generally need a rather large house so characters can move about, providing natural scene breaks and changes in environment to help keep audiences from becoming too restless.[18]

With a short film, on the other hand, having events unfold in a single location often makes perfect sense. This allows for ease in shooting since the crew doesn't have to tear down and set-up equipment in multiple sites, but it also represents an opportunity for the storyteller behind the film to truly focus on characters. A single well-selected and well-dressed location can be profoundly effective. A perfect example of this is the short film "Those Unattended," by director Brian Garvey.[19] This sci-fi family drama unfolds in a single dinning room. Production design, lighting, and visual effects all help instantly drop us into this futuristic world. We never leave this one room during the six minutes of the film. But given the mind's natural propensity to fill in implied information beyond the edges of the frame, we effectively assume

---

[17] *Writing Short Films* by Linda J. Cowgirl, Watson-Guptill Publications, 2005. Page 113.

[18] A recent notable exception to this is the film *Buried*, directed by Rodrigo Cortés and starring Ryan Reynolds alone in a wooden box after his character has been buried alive by insurgents in the Middle East. Even this film doesn't risk overstaying its welcome and clocks in at 95-minutes.

[19] "Those Unattended", written and directed by Brian Garvey, 2014. www.briangarveyfilms.com

a very similar world exists in the rest of their house, their neighborhood, their city, and so forth. Garvey's film is a perfect example of the new wave of short films embracing brevity by honing in on characters' relationships within the confines of limited time and space. I highly recommend putting this book down for six minutes and hopping on to Garvey's website or Vimeo and watching "Those Unattended."

I have experimented with this singular location approach for a while. Even as far back as my first successful short film, "Cellar Door,"[20] I creatively utilized an apple orchard as a singular location (other than the opening credits sequence) by making it a character within the story. As I've mentioned before, however, that film was thirty-seven minutes and even though it was accepted into festivals at the time, as we will discuss in later chapters, that runtime is no longer a viable length for a short film today.

More recently, I have directed films like "Playing with Ice,"[21] which focuses on an interview for a strange scientific project. The interview probes into the difficult past of the main character within the context of this interview room. "Intrigue,"[22] is another short I wrote and directed that features two characters in a room. Even with a six-minute running time and confined to a single dinning room, the film effectively flips genres midway through for a fun twist. I have also served the producer and cinematographer for other projects that unfold in similar ways, such as "A Regular Haunt,"[23] which is a comedy about two roommates in a house that

---

[20] "Cellar Door," directed by Mikel J. Wisler, 2007.

[21] "Playing with Ice," 2013. Available at www.StoriesByTheRiver.org.

[22] "Intrigue," 2015. Available at www.StoriesByTheRiver.org.

[23] "A Regular Haunt," written by Audrey Noone and directed by Christopher Grace, 2015. Available at www.StoriesByTheRiver.org.

may be haunted, as events unfold in real time (less than five minutes, in fact).

While I have often used a single location as means to embrace brevity in my filmmaking, it is by no means the only method for making effective short films. The crucial idea is that whether your short film has one or many locations, be sure that your story is focused and free from any excess exposition or material that hinders the forward momentum of the story. Establishing a new location in a film that is only a few minutes long may be too much of a distraction.

The challenge with any such short film is finding the right premise and entrance into the story, but this challenge doesn't have to prove impossible. As more and more filmmakers are demonstrating, there seems to be no end for how to accomplish all of this and thus, tell a compelling story, even if we only see one location and the film lasts mere minutes.

Go Visual

The other trend I have observed and experienced first hand is that a large number of successful short films these days are often very light on dialogue. Harkening back to the early days of cinema, many new filmmakers embrace the challenge of relying strictly on visuals to tell their story. This can be counterintuitive to new filmmakers raised on a steady diet of dialogue-heavy feature films and television. Dialogue is a wonderful tool, and if you look at the vast majority of the films I've written and directed, you'll notice I do enjoy working with dialogue. However, dialogue is also one of the hardest aspects of scriptwriting to master. It takes practice and lots of development. It can be easy for new filmmakers to be lured into the trap of making an early project that relies exclusively on dialogue to tell its story. And, why not? All you need to do is point the camera at your actors and let them do the work, right? Then, you cut it together and you have a movie, right? That almost never goes well.

A few years ago, I attended two different film festivals, back to back, where I saw a feature film that embodied this faulty logic and lazy filmmaking. These two separate and unrelated features displayed the folly of attempting to rely exclusively on dialogue to tell a story.[24] Specifically, both of these films displayed a clear desire by the filmmakers to emulate the style of dialogue writing made famous by Kevin Smith.[25] Both films were excruciatingly boring visually—and in every other way imaginable—and felt flat given their derivative nature. One was even so horribly shot and edited that it was hard to believe it had been accepted to any festival. No thought had been given to the fact that movies are a visual medium. I can sincerely say those are roughly four hours of my life I desperately wish I could have back!

Making such mediocre films could have been avoided if the filmmakers had invested more time in embracing brevity and developing their skills in visual storytelling, which is another reason why I believe short films offer a great training ground for new filmmakers. Looking at the films that make a splash today, they are incredibly visual. I highly recommend checking out any of the short films nominated for Oscars™ each year. These are carefully shot and edited films that take seriously the visual nature of cinema. So much can be communicated within the

---

[24] I won't mention the titles, but it wouldn't really matter, as both films have long faded into obscurity.

[25] Including *Clerks* (1994), *Mallrats* (1995), *Dogma* (1999), and *Red State* (2011).

frame that dialogue is often unnecessary for many of the new short films being made.

I experimented with this approach with my short film, "Stop."[26] The film remains my most successful short film to date both in terms of festival reception and plays on Vimeo and YouTube. I would attribute this in large part to its short running time (just over eight minutes) and nearly dialogue-free execution, after the opening scene. The film eventually grabbed the attention of an independent production company in Los Angeles. They contacted me to discuss the possibilities of developing the short film into a feature.

I do not mean to suggest that new short films need to be made exclusively sans dialogue, but I do think the challenge is one that is worth contemplating, if you are new to filmmaking and want to develop your visual and technical skills. Nonetheless, the undeniable reality is that audiences today are incredibly sophisticated. With increasingly accessible digital filmmaking technology, more polished and cinematic-looking short films are becoming readily available to viewers. As a result, even the expectations from the casual viewer of short films on YouTube are that short films will be visually compelling. No exceptions!

In the next chapter, I will look at how this trend developed so that we can better understand what factors influence the viewing of our short films. As you come to understand these factors, you will be better equipped to make films that grab the viewer's attention and keep it.

---

[26] Written & directed by Wisler, 2011. Available at www.mikelwisler.com.

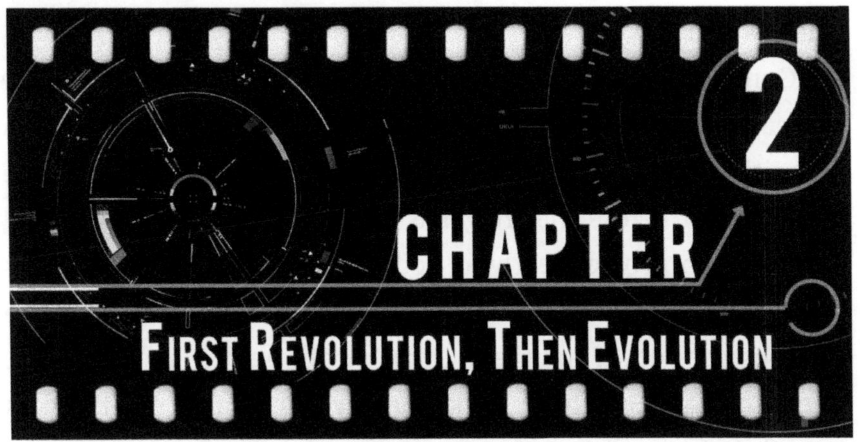

Have you seen the short film "Tune for Two?"[27] Seriously, put this book down right now and go watch it! It's cool, I'll wait. Even if you have seen it before, it's worth taking a look at it again. It is only two minutes and forty-one seconds long.

Now that you've seen it, we can carry on (seriously, I hope you watched it as it is quite important to what I'm going to explore here).

"Tune for Two" is a perfect example of what the new landscape of short films looks like. There is no dialogue at all. The exposition is communicated entirely by visual methods. We are dropped into a situation where we can quickly grasp what is going on, but no time at all is spent on backstory. We have no idea who the hit man is and why he has been called upon to assassinate the poor man he drags out into this snowy field. In fact, we have no idea if this is business or personal. Maybe the man at the end of the gun did something and this hit man (though maybe he's not a hit man at all, but he sure seems to behave like one) just wants to kill him. Either way, what could this poor guy possibly have done to deserve execution in the middle of a field? We just don't know.

---

[27] Written and directed by Gunnar Järvstad, 2011. https://vimeo.com/21362582

And that's perfect!

Gunnar Järvstad, the filmmaker behind this film, clearly grasped that the film he was making would only be hurt by such exposition. The point is not the "why." The point here is the moment just before the trigger is pulled. It is a shared moment between two people clearly at odds and after the moment fades away, whatever choices have led them to this moment come crashing back down and the hit man carries out the assassination. The film has a definite dark comedy tone, and yet there is something about it that moves me. The short ends with the dead man being buried. Just as we did not get backstory, we also do not get to see any fallout from this moment. And yet, I can't help but wonder how this hit man might forever be haunted, possibly even changed, by the moment we just witnessed. And that is the power of a truly great short film: it invites and sometimes even demands the viewer's continued participation, since clearly there is so much more to the story than what we have witnessed in mere minutes.

So, how did we get here when many short films used to be "mini-features" that ran thirty or forty minutes, like the projects in the 1989 collection of short films by various directors called New York Stories?[28] A rapid evolution has taken place in the medium of short films in the last several years and understanding why these dramatic changes have taken place will help us in the coming years. Understand how we can make the most of these changes and how we can foresee new changes that allow us to define the short films to come.

With all of this in mind, let's take a look at how we got here.

---

[28] *New York Stories*, directed by Woody Allen, Francis Ford Coppola, and Martin Scorsese, 1989. http://www.imdb.com/title/tt0097965/

The Digital Revolution

If you follow filmmaking and videography magazines, blogs, and forums, you know that much has been made of the digital revolution that has introduced affordable new filmmaking technology. As a result, I have no interest in going into detailed information about any of that here. However, if you find you need a good primer on how filmmaking has changed because of the rapid introduction of high quality digital tools, I highly recommend the insightful documentary produced by Keanu Reeves called *Side by Side.*[29]

For our purposes here, it is important only to note a few key things about the digital revolution. First of all, where the tools required for making a film (cameras, lights, film stock, etc.) were once quite expensive (even prohibitively expensive for many wanting to break into filmmaking), digital technology has been a democratizing force. As is the trend in most industries, there is always a constant pressure to produce cheaper materials and tools that drive down the production costs, which allows a business to competitively price their products. With an increased adoption of new technologies, those new technologies also become cheaper to mass-produce. The cheaper and more abundant such tools become, the more people are equipped to do things they might not have been able to do before, like making a movie.

This is exactly what has taken place within the film industry. Whereas it once took tens to hundreds of thousands of dollars just for the technical aspects of making a small indie film, today, with

29 *Side by Side,* directed by Christopher Kenneally, 2012. www.imdb.com/title/tt2014338

a few hundred dollars and a personal computer, anyone can own a digital camera capable of shooting remarkably cinematic footage and edit it. The tools, once only available to professionals with serious funding, are now accessible in various forms and often, at consumer prices. The effects of the digital revolution is ongoing as cameras, lenses, editing tools, and even lighting gear continue to get cheaper and better. Even smartphones that most of us carry around are capable of making some remarkable images if one knows how best to use them.[30]

One thing has not changed: filmmaking is a craft that requires intense practice to achieve proficiency. The digital revolution has provided amazing new opportunities to people like me who do not have the financial means to even attempt making films in the celluloid-based industry of decades past. Even though this is wonderful news, there are also drawbacks:

"While the ease of being able to make films on low-cost digital video equipment has increased the quantity of independent movies being made today," writes Phil Hall in his book *Independent Film Distribution*, "it has had an opposite effect on the quality of such films. To be frank, there is a lopsided ratio of quality to quantity."[31]

Jon Popick, an online magazine editor for *Planet Sick-Boy*, had this to say about what results he has witnessed from the digital revolution:

> The fact that any schlub can walk into a Wal-Mart and buy a digital video camera for a couple of hundred bucks

---

[30] As I write this, Sundance Film Festival has just finished screening their first feature film shot entirely with iPhones and lens adaptors.

[31] *Independent Film Distribution* by Phil Hall, Michael Wise Productions, © 2006 Phil Hall. Page 42.

> means that anybody can make their own *Blair Witch* later that day, in their backyard with their drunk friends. Ten years ago, the only people who would try something like this were pretty serious about what they were doing. It's possible a few revolutionary filmmakers get their big breaks this way, but it's mostly going to produce a whole lot of garbage. I picture film festival programmers putting guns in their mouths after a few weeks of watching these movies.[32]

Did he just use the word "garbage?" You bet! No one sets out to make garbage, but if you're not careful, you just might. A mentality that has been propagated by some filmmakers who have made it into the Hollywood system is that if you want to make a film, you should "Just do it." To some degree, they are right. Nevertheless, there remains a right way to "just do it", and there are plenty of wrongs ways (or at least problematic ways).

I often meet people or see film projects made by people who have not taken the time to truly develop the craftsmanship of good storytelling or learned the technical excellence required to make films well. Too many novice filmmakers assume that because their sweet new camera can achieve a cinematic look, their film project will automatically look "professional" (or worse, that it will magically make them a professional filmmaker). Too often I have seen such projects fall flat for lack of a real understanding and appreciation for good lighting, effective framing, shooting for the edit, directing actors, and selecting a worthwhile story to tell in the first place (the worst cinematic sin

---

[32] *Independent Film Distribution* by Phil Hall, Michael Wise Productions, © 2006 Phil Hall. Pages 42-43.

as far as I'm concerned). The 'moral': Just because you have professional tools at your disposal does not mean your project will automatically be good. You need to know how to use the tools and really hone the craft.

In fact, I once worked on the crew of a feature that was shot on 35mm film with a professional crew. A lot of money was spent on the project. But in the end, I found the film to be painfully boring to sit through. Now maybe I was too harsh on the film (though I really don't think so), but here are my reasons for disliking it so much: I feel it failed, in large part, due to the fact that the composition of each shot was uninspired (mostly medium close-ups with characters in center frame) and the camera never moved. I was told that the director and DP chose this static camera shooting style so as not to overdramatize the story. However, given that the whole film was almost entirely one long dialogue scene after another, a little over dramatization might have helped it not fall incredibly flat.[33] I found this especially disappointing since the following year I worked on the crew of a different feature film that was made for far less money. It was shot digitally, though the tools at the time were rather cumbersome, but we were able to shoot a far more visually compelling film that was dynamic and engaging.

Again, I bring this up to make this point: just because technology is capable of providing great results does not mean that those great results will happen automatically. Regardless of

---

[33] Note that I have not named this film and I do not wish to disparage anyone's good efforts in making a film, as I know it is hard work. What I express above are only my opinions as a fellow filmmaker with potentially differing aesthetic values. I learned a great deal being part of that crew and the experience has proved invaluable! However, I would be dishonest if I said I felt the film turned out well, as I believe it represents a missed opportunity to embrace the visual nature of cinematic storytelling.

what cinematic tools are at your disposal, good results ultimately come from having a solid story combined with craftsmanship and good aesthetic sensibilities. There are no short cuts!

The second challenge that the digital revolution has presented for filmmakers is that now there are so many more of us. The democratization of filmmaking means that virtually anyone can make a film, especially a short film. This is great news! And, it's also sort of bad news too. It is good news because it means new filmmakers have a shot at making a beautiful short film, even if their financial resources are incredibly limited. It is simultaneously bad news because it means that the world is now saturated with films from new filmmakers. There are a lot of short films out there. Many, possibly most, are not all that good, if I'm being honest.

Is this a reason to be discouraged? No! Again, I come back to my above point that a good story combined with craftsmanship and good aesthetic sensibilities is the best way to go about making a great film (short or feature). In the coming pages we will examine together some principles of visual storytelling, particularly in short films, and then we will walk away from this examination better equipped to critically evaluate our work and be better prepared to stand out in an increasingly media-saturated world.

Before we examine how to overcome media saturation, there is a final aspect of the digital revolution we need to address: the Internet. Short films have always struggled to find an audience in the United States. Canada and many European nations often show short films on TV or have cable stations that carry short films as part of their programming. I have sold some of my short films to such stations, but in the last decade the Internet has been a game changer: it connects new audiences to short films.

When YouTube appeared nearly a decade ago, no one knew for sure what the future would hold, but as increasingly better digital cameras became available to new filmmakers, YouTube (and eventually Vimeo and many other such sites) became the primary way short film creators could get their content out to audiences. The gatekeepers between filmmakers and audiences were bypassed completely.

YouTube has also exerted its own unintentional influence on filmmakers and short films because they have changed how we watch short films. Ultimately, this influence is the source of the profound changes in how short films are being made today. In other words, YouTube has changed short films forever! Many new filmmakers have adapted intuitively, but for many of us, a deeper understanding of how this change happened and what it means for short film creators today might be highly beneficial.

Shorts Got Shorter

Short films have definitely gotten shorter. The 'culprits' behind these shrinking runtimes are YouTube, Facebook, Twitter, and other similar sites. With the increasing use of video and social media sites as little detours during working hours, or an easy distraction during a commute, or when just killing time at home, the demand for quick and short content has taken off. Videos that go viral tend to be incredibly short. This is both true in storytelling forms like narrative and documentary short films, but it is also quite true of marketing materials. I have been working in video production for as long as I have been a filmmaker and I have worked in various roles creating short content for companies that tell their stories quickly and elegantly. These have ranged from smaller local clients to larger clients, such as the set of several YouTube videos for New Balance® when they launched their new line of sports bras (each was less than 50 seconds).[34] Those videos went on to win a Telly Award.

The point is, whether pitching a product or offering a bit of entertainment, content creators have generally come to understand that shorter is better. There are so many distractions on the Internet and the impulse is quite strong to click on to the next thing or scroll further down one's Twitter or Facebook feeds. As filmmakers have begun to think more about what will engage an audience on YouTube rather than an audience at a film festival, short films have naturally gotten quite short. Think back to "Tune for Two".

I can hear protests already that not all short films are that short. While true, effective short films that tend to go viral or at least garner serious online viewership consistently come in under ten minutes. Also, keep in mind that everything in our lives seems to be moving to the Internet. There's no getting around the need to think in terms of how to connect with your online audience. A great example of an effective short film is the Tropefest Winner from 2013, "Cargo."[35] Here is another short film you're going to want to stop right now and watch.

Did you watch it? You'll notice that there is almost no dialogue in the film. No exposition needed. Once we see the man's wife in the car, we know exactly what's going on thanks to

---

[34] I served as cinematographer for those videos, which were produced by the talented folks at Real Cool Productions. http://www.realcooltv.com.

[35] "Cargo," directed by Ben Howling & Yolanda Ramke, 2013. https://vimeo.com/56629974

the general audience's familiarity with the zombie genre. After that, it's all drama as the father does all he can to save his child. The film is seven minutes long, but contains an incredible depth in being able to use an arguably tired genre to communicate the level of love and sacrifice that would drive a man to give up the last moments of his life to save his child—as a matter of fact, to think past his own life and do what he can to give his child the best chances for survival. I still cannot re-watch this short film without breaking into tears! It is no wonder the film picked-up 5.6 million views on the Tropefest YouTube Channel during it's run in that online festival. It continues to garner views to this day, so yes, not everything is as short as "Tune for Two.", but the reality is that very few short films longer than 15 minutes receive a lot of attention online.

This reality has also affected film festivals. I mentioned earlier that the indie film world is saturated with short films now thanks to the digital revolution. What this means is that film festivals have more submissions than ever before, and the projects that manage to display brevity and eloquence tend to be the ones getting in. Sure, many festivals still accept submissions for short films up to forty minutes in length (or what I tend to call "no man's land" because they are too long to be considered short films and they are not nearly long enough to be a feature), but the reality is that when I go to festivals, I just don't see those films included in the lineup. I see five, ten, fifteen, and maybe a twenty-minute short, if it's really remarkable.

How filmmakers are accomplishing this brevity is to abandon the need to make the "mini-feature" into a short film. At the end of the day, yes, even "Tune for Two" has a basic three act structure at work within it (a problem is introduced: a hit man is about to kill someone; conflict: the mark starts to sing a Sesame Street/Muppets tune that's too catchy not to sing along to; resolution: when the song ends the hit man pulls the trigger), but these are all things that happen within the context of one scene. There is no need for backstory. There is no set-up and payoff. There are no lengthy scenes of dialogue.

Think of "Cargo." The temptation might be to give some hint as to how the zombie apocalypse happened, or at least try to indicate how the wife was infected, which might also include showing how the car accident happened. In a feature film, yes, we would need to see these things, but in this new age of short films, we want to be dropped right into the story as quickly as possible. And, in this sense, short films almost function more like scenes taken from a larger story. The old mantra for screenwriting is that for any scene in a feature screenplay, we should come in late and leave early. The writer should provide only enough information that propels the story forward and then move on.[36] Short films, now more than ever, function the same way which is why many short films now seem to capture a crucial moment in a character's life rather than seek to show a whole character arc.

To that end, short films tend to rely heavily on visual storytelling to invoke things such as cultural icons and genre expectations seen in our two examples. We do not need to know anything about the two men in the field in "Tune for Two." Most of us are quite familiar, thanks to other movies, with the general concept of a hit man. Again, thanks to other movies and/or books, hardly anyone is devoid of awareness of what zombies are and what the general rules of a zombie story entail. Therefore, a short

---

[36] Ever wonder why no one seems to say "goodbye" and then hang up at the end of phone calls in movies?

film like "Cargo" can skip the exposition to focus on visuals that tell the real story of the film: parental love means a willingness to look out for your child even as you die yourself. So, the filmmakers reveal to us visually that these three people involved in a car accident were in fact a family via the car window sticker and dialogue. The rest of the film plays out in actions as the father takes steps to do what he can to help his child reach safety. The ending of the film is powerful precisely because there is so little dialogue. Actions and reactions tell us everything we need to know.

In my own short film, "Intrigue," I relied a lot on audiences' general familiarity with spy movies and the characters that tend to inhabit such stories. By doing so, I could drop right into a rendezvous between two spies without having to spend any time actually introducing them as spies. In fact, the whole short film, which is only six minutes long (available to view for free at www.storiesbytheriver.org), is designed around audiences' expectations about how spies are "supposed" to behave. For this reason, as the film progresses, people quickly catch that maybe these two characters aren't exactly what they claim to be. In this sense, I leaned into genre expectations in order to create humor, but this need not only apply to a comedic short film. Creative storytellers employ many methods to play off of audience expectations and, by doing so; they craft better ways to generate suspense and surprise as well as more cathartic scenes of comedy and drama.

As filmmakers have sought to tell their stories in shorter run times, the pacing has picked up. This does not mean that cutting is always frantic, but it does mean that process shots (ie: a character opens the door to her apartment and walks in) that might usually be part of a feature film are not included in a short film unless they are truly essential to telling the story. Such pacing can be determined by a writer carefully thinking ahead of time about the brevity of a short film, as well as the need to shoot quickly. This is often the case with shorts, so there is no point in wasting time on set getting the shots that won't make the cut anyway. If that ends up not being the case with a short script, one hopes the editor has some sense of brevity and chops out any dead weight from a short film!

Film Festivals & YouTube

For decades, short films were something seen only at festivals with strictly limited play in other venues on rare occasions. For the most part, average moviegoers or television viewers never saw short films. This meant that as a filmmaker making a short film, your one and only hope was to get into several festivals (preferably the big ones) and impress the right people so you could move on to making feature films that people might actually get to watch. No wonder filmmakers have long seen short films not as a means to genuinely connect with an audience or tell a compelling story so much as a means to prove they have filmmaking chops. Some European nations do run some short films on television stations, but in America at least; there was little hope of reaching audiences outside of festivals with a short film.[37]

Not so today. One of the democratizing effects of the Internet

[37] The Sundance Channel and IFC are known to run short films, but these generally are short films that have made their mark in the festival circuit first.

is that it has directly connected filmmakers and audiences. Don't get me wrong, it is still incredibly hard to stand out and actually grab people's attention on the Internet due to the sheer volume of content that is created each day. Options are virtually endless.

The number of film festivals has been on the rise as more people try their hand at filmmaking and seek a means to make connections that might enable a film career. But, as noted by people in the industry for a few years now, even when it comes to selling a feature film, few distribution deals are made at film festivals any more.[38] With the exception of the big four (Sundance, Toronto, Cannes, SXSW), the reality is that distributors just do not bother attending most festivals any more.

Meanwhile, more film festivals seem to be launched each year. What this suggests to me is that the purpose film festivals serve is changing. Especially when it comes to short films, it is now quite unrealistic to expect that getting into festivals will get Hollywood executives or distributors to see your work and come talk to you about making more films. They simply are not in attendance. On the other hand, if your goals are to get your film in front of indie film enthusiasts, share it with audiences that will see your work projected on a large screen and not on a smartphone, and networking with other filmmakers, there are now more opportunities than ever. However, it just might cost you a lot of money.

Again, I come back to the concept of market saturation, or what former WIRED Magazine editor, Chris Anderson, refers to as "lack of scarcity" in his book, *Free: The Future of a Radical Price*.[39]

---

[38] For detailed information on this change in film festivals, see *The Art of Film Funding: Alternative Financing Concepts* by Carole Lee Dean, 2007, Michael Wiese Productions.

[39] *Free: The Future of a Radical Price* by Chris Anderson, Hyperion eBook, 2009.

In economic terms, the supply of short films far outweighs the demand at film festivals: there is a significant surplus of short films when compared to the limited number of film festival slots available. As a result, the vast majority of festivals today can afford to be exceptionally picky about what they select. So to give your film the best shot at exposure over as many festivals as possible, it means having to play the odds. Chances are that even with a good film on your hands, between sixty to ninety percent or more of the film festivals you submit to will reject your film. With the average cost of film festival submissions ranging from $20 to $40 for short films, it doesn't take a whole lot of submissions before a filmmaker can be out several hundred to a couple thousand dollars before even getting a single acceptance or rejection email.[40]

As a filmmaker who has submitted to hundreds of film festivals over the years and has played at dozens, I have personal awareness of how things have changed over the last ten years. Not that long ago, my thirty-seven minute short film got into two regional festivals. Shortly after that, my thirty-minute film made it into five national and one international film festivals and even picked up some nominations and an award. My most recent projects that include a twenty-minute film, an eleven-minute film, and a six-minute film, have gathered an awful lot of rejections. My newer films have gotten into some festivals, but not that many and only after submitting to a large number of festivals. In fact, I have found that when submitting to the same festivals where I have played previously with my longer films, my

---

Thanks to Eric Bumpus for bringing this insightful book to my attention.

[40] And that is if you get any response. In my experience there are plenty of festivals that are rather lousy at sending out any notification at all, which, frankly, I find incredibly inconsiderate.

newer and shorter films still struggle to be accepted.

It was 2008 and 2009 when my thirty-minute psychological thriller, “Cold October”, played at six festivals. I was still new to the festival submission process at the time and so I used a festival submission service. I paid for the service and they researched and submitted the film to festivals for me. Often, due to their connections, fees were reduced or waved completely. “Cold October” was submitted to 75 film festivals. I paid $2,307 for those 75 submissions. This means that since the film got into six festivals, 69 festivals rejected the film. That’s a 92% rejection rate, or only an 8% acceptance rate. Another way to look at it is to average the total cost by the number of successful festival selections, which means I spent $384.50 per selection. No matter how you look at it, it was a lot of money for very little in return. I’ve never used a festival submission service again as I ultimately do not feel they were as selective in their festival choices as I would have hoped.

From 2011 to 2012, I submitted my short film, “Stop”, to a mere fourteen film festivals. It was accepted at five. I spent a total of $455 on festival submissions. With nine out of fourteen festivals rejecting the film that means I had a 64% rejection rate. In other words, I had a whopping 36% acceptance rate, which blows away the 8% acceptance rate for “Cold October”. It also means I only spent $91 per official selection. Many factors may play into why the acceptance rate is so much higher for “Stop” than for “Cold October”, but it seems noteworthy to me that “Stop” is only slightly longer than eight minutes whereas “Cold October” is a solid thirty minutes. I was also far more selective in the types of festivals for which I submitted “Stop” so as to maximize my chances of being accepted.

Following "Stop", I made "A Silent Universe", which has a total running time of twenty-five minutes. I was not yet convinced of the need to keep my short films shorter. I learned the hard way that the festival market had changed. Even as I very selectively submitted the film to a total of twenty festivals, "A Silent Universe" was only selected by two. Two selections out of twenty submissions is a 90% rejection rate.[41] It is possible that "Stop" is a better film than "A Silent Universe" and this accounts for the reason why so few festivals selected the latter. However, "A Silent Universe" was nominated for two Maverick Movie Awards in writing and visual effects. I also produced another twenty-five short film that same year that only managed to play at one film festival (where it was voted the regional audience favorite). The general reaction by audiences has been that these films are good, but that hasn't translated into the kind of festival selection rate "Stop" garnered.

Even "Playing with Ice", the twenty-minute film I directed in 2013, hasn't faired too well domestically, playing in only two US festivals while managing to play at five festivals overseas. I did change my strategy for submissions slightly. I first submitted the film to a few larger festivals, knowing full well my chances of getting in were slim. I then chose a few mid-range festivals and followed up those submissions by eventually submitting the film to a whole lot of free festivals, and a few smaller festivals with $5 submission fees. In the end, I submitted "Playing with Ice" to a total of 46 festivals but only spent a grand total of $338 on all my submissions, which is less than the per-selection average for

---

[41] I was invited by filmmakers I'd met through social media to screen "A Silent Universe" at a special film festival event they were hosting, but I am not including it in this analysis as it was not a selective festival open to general submissions.

"Cold October". That comes out to a rejection rate of 89%, which is nearly identical to "A Silent Universe."

My more recent short films are still undergoing festival submissions at this point, making it too early to try to conduct any conclusive analysis of the data they are generating, but a few things are becoming clear to me. My experience as well as the conversations I've had with other filmmakers indicates that short films over the ten-minute mark face much higher rejection rates by film festivals today.

In speaking with fellow filmmakers about the current climate of film festivals and whether or not they ultimately continue to benefit filmmakers, it seems to me that the tide of filmmaker opinion is changing when it comes to festivals. With new platforms like FilmFreeway[42] that handle submissions for many festivals with free entries, I sincerely believe that a major shift may be about to happen for film festivals. You might even say that the short film festival bubble is about to burst. Many filmmakers I know, myself included, no longer consider festival submission fees to be a worthwhile investment,[43] at least in any significant amount, when filmmakers can reach out directly to their audience on YouTube, Facebook, Twitter, and Vimeo.

A strong argument can be made for bypassing festivals altogether (or at least the costly mid-range festivals) by simply investing the money that would have gone to submission fees into online marketing, especially now that YouTube allows content creators the ability to share in revenue from ads on their site. A

---

[42] http://filmfreeway.com.

[43] One filmmaker I know told me that given the genre movies she's been making, she's better off attending game and comic book conventions and selling copies of the film rather than trying to get into festivals. Makes sense to me. She can make money, which is hardly ever the case with most festivals.

savvy filmmaker with the right short film and a solid plan for reaching his or her target audience might well be better off with such an approach. The upside is that far more people are likely to see the film online and the filmmaker might be able to eventually recover some or all of the money invested in the marketing. The possibility of reaching a break-even point and receiving a positive return on investment at least exists in such a scenario. That is not the case when it comes to being selected by or even winning awards at most mid-range film festivals. Even if a filmmaker doesn't take this kind of approach, I think it is worth considering the opportunity costs involved, such as the benefits or losses realized from other areas that could gain the filmmaker far more exposure than playing at mid-range film festivals.

Furthermore, getting into small and mid-sized festivals does not mean a whole lot to the gatekeepers of the film industry. Allow me to offer up this personal anecdote: A few years ago I attended the American Film Market (AFM) where I met with several companies in an effort to raise funding for a feature film. In my pitch package for the project was a list of my previous short films and all the many film festival laurels I had accumulated to that point. I observed in meeting after meeting that all those festivals didn’t seem to constitute good enough of a track record to help get the film funded: my producing partner and I walked away empty handed. At a glance, my suspicion is that these producers and distributors we were pitching to could not find Sundance or Toronto on my list and all those other festivals laurels were essentially meaningless. Oh sure, they acted mildly impressed, some even commenting that it looked like we were getting into a lot of festivals. But, again, we still walked away empty handed. All those laurels might have filled me with pride, but they did not instill the confidence needed by any of those companies to justify taking a risk on our feature film project. Now I cannot say for a fact that if I had a Sundance laurel on my pitch package that someone would have funded the project. Obviously, there are many factors at play here, but I can't help but suspect that if I had such a recognizable festival name in my list of official selections for past projects that some of those conversations might have gone very differently.

As a result of this experience, I began rethinking my approach to film festivals over the following years. As difficult and depressing as it might be to admit this, I wasted a lot of money on festival submissions. I realize this may step on the toes of a lot of festival organizers out there, particularly mid-size festivals with short film submission fees in the twenty to thirty dollar range, but I sincerely no longer see the value of spending my hard-earned dollars on submission fees for such festivals—at least not in any significant volume and for some projects, not at all.

Please allow me to share a little with you about my own experiences with playing at film festivals in recent years. I realize that this may come across as rather negative, but I hope I am able to make my point clearly. While not all of my experiences with festivals have been negative (some in fact have been incredibly rewarding), I have noticed a pattern that has caused me to continue to rethink how I approach submitting my films to festivals (and whether or not I attend festivals even when selected).

My 2011 short film, "Stop", was an experiment in making a project with Internet viewers as the target audience. I released the film immediately to Vimeo and YouTube. Film festival submissions only happened later, and almost as an afterthought.

It managed to get into a few festivals and picked up an award from the Maverick Movie Awards and the Boston Science Fiction Film Festival.[44] A year after releasing the film online I was approached about potentially developing "Stop" into a feature film, and not because of any of the festivals it played at or awards it had won: it was because the film had been spotted on YouTube. The company that reached out to me simply found the film online. As of this publication, the film has over 25,000 views on YouTube. That is far from viral, but also means far more people have seen my humble sci-fi thriller than would have if I had only submitted it to festivals. In fact, I recall the utterly demoralizing experience at a festival where I sat through a screening of a block of short films, which included "Stop", only to realize that other than two or three festival staff, I was the only other person in the theater. No one else (audience or other filmmakers) had shown up. In that instance, I happened to have also wasted gas money since the festival was out of state.

I have also had the experience with a different festival where they changed the schedule at the last minute but never updated the schedule on the festival's website. I showed up with a couple of friends for where the screening of "Stop" should have taken place. We found a locked theater. Another filmmaker, his own short film selected and supposedly playing in the same block as mine, was there too. Finally, we managed to get our hands on an updated printed schedule that clearly indicated our films were not playing that day but on some other day. I had other plans for that day and could not attend the actual screening of "Stop" at that

---

[44] Winner of The Precious Award for the film's twist ending at the 2011 Maverick Movie Awards. Note that MMA is not a film festival but an indie film award organization. At the 2012 Boston Sci-fi Film Festival, "Stop" was awarded Best New England Short Film.

festival.

These types of experiences, and many more I would rather not share here, have led me to a fundamental rethinking of what the real value and role of film festivals are in my long-term goals as a filmmaker. All of that money I have spent on festival submissions could have been spent on new gear or maybe more importantly, on paying my crew and cast even for small projects. To be clear, I do still submit to festivals, but I am extremely selective now. I am willing to submit to festivals with incredibly low or free entry fees because the risk is minimal. If I'm just looking to collect some festival laurels and get a project in front of indie-film-loving audiences, this seems like the more frugal way to do it. Otherwise, I might save my dollars and submit to a handful of the big festivals when I have a project on my hands that I feel has a potential shot at getting in. It is a calculated risk I don't take lightly, making sure submissions to such festivals are few, so as not to quickly spend thousands of dollars. Meanwhile, I can't help but come back to the fact that it was not any of the awards or nominations or the several festivals that "Stop" played at that ultimately got me into conversations with a production company wanting to develop that short film into a feature. It was the mere presence of the film online. What's more, I don't think I'm alone in this type of experience.

For this reason, I believe things are changing dramatically for film festivals. For one, they now have to compete with the online world and one way to compete is to try to schedule as many filmmakers as possible in order to make the festival as broad-reaching as possible. But rather than risk burning out audiences by simply adding more days to a festival's duration, festivals are trying to schedule more films into the same amount of screen time. Therefore, short films longer than ten or fifteen minutes are almost impossible to have selected by most festivals these days as festival organizers seek to cram as many shorts as possible into every screening block. More and more online film festivals (The Online Film Festival, New Media Film Festival, Onecloudfest, and others) are emerging in an effort to combine the power of social networking sites like Facebook and the ease of reaching a global audience. But, the films that do well at these festivals are also quite short, like "Cargo."

I do believe in the value of smaller festivals when it comes to regional exposure and networking with other indie filmmakers. In fact, this is the reason I helped launch the Stories by the River Film Festival, as a means to celebrate and give exposure to new filmmakers in the New England area and encourage them to connect with each other. We give out a cash prize for the audience favorite film and provide a variety of refreshments. We know how quickly festival submissions can add up, so we purposefully keep our submission fee as low as possible.[45]

I've also had the privilege to serve as a judge on the Digi60 Filmmakers' Festival out of Ottawa, Ontario. Digi60 is a particularly unique festival in that local filmmakers make two-and-a-half-minute short films specifically for the festival and judges offer specific feedback about what works and what doesn't for each film. It is geared directly at providing valuable insights and hands-on experience for new filmmakers and the two-and-a-half-minute maximum length is amazing training for making

---

[45] We experimented with a free submission model for one year, but found that we had to deal with far too many blind submission from filmmakers who had not taken the time to read our guidelines, which clearly spelled out that we were looking for films with a New England connection. We had to go back to charging a small fee that reimburses some expenses.

focused and effecting short films. I really enjoyed being on the judging panel. Experiences like these remind me that there is a real value to regional festivals!

Ultimately, you must examine your goals in submitting to a festival; how much you are willing to spend, the type of festival, the amount of networking, the chance of being picked up for something more, and the possibility of awards vary greatly. I do sense that change is on the horizon for many midrange festivals, though, as more and more filmmakers recognize the limited return on investment that often is the case with general festival submissions. As short films themselves change, there is an important question you have to ask yourself: “Are festivals, as we have known them for decades, still the ideal end goal for your short films?”

The digital distribution revolution means that short films have gotten shorter due to audience expectations from content provided online, but it also means that short films have gotten better. This is great news for audiences, but it also means there are some serious challenges for new filmmakers to keep in mind as they embark on making short films. We will tackle those challenges next.

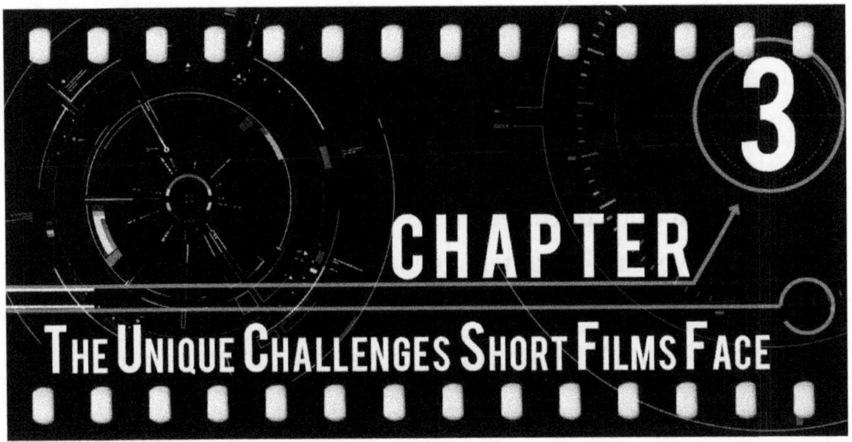

I recognize that this chapter could be read as a bit of a downer. I do not intend it as such. Rather, I hope this will serve as a means of confronting realistically the challenges that short films face today. As a result, I believe new filmmakers will be better equipped to innovatively think about short films, rising to meet and defeat these challenges, and leading us into the next wave of short film evolution. Now, with this in mind, I have no intention of sugarcoating any of what follows. I hope you'll bear with me as we identify and understand exactly what the challenges are. It is imperative that we first grasp the unique challenges faced by short films in order to develop creative solutions. In Chapter Four, we will address how to embrace these challenges in an effort to make the most effective short films today.

Quality is a Foregone Conclusion

Short films today do not get any automatic passes or excuses for being made on minimal budgets or no budgets at all. As with feature films, the predominant expectation of general audiences is that short films will have a high level of production quality. It matters little if a project is small or a major Hollywood production. The reality is that technology has developed to a degree where inexpensive equipment can emulate the cinematic look that traditionally had been relegated to multi-million dollar studio productions until recently.

Now, if you are a camera technology nerd (as I am), you are well aware that there are definite differences that separate a Canon or Nikon DSLR or Sony mirrorless camera from an ARRI Alexa or RED Epic or 35mm Kodak film stock. However, all other things being equal (or at least assuming good directing and shooting) the average viewer is not able to discern the difference between a film shot on a DSLR (*Like Crazy*[46] or *Act of Valor*[47]) or a RED Epic (*Prometheus*[48] or *Captain America: The Winter Soldier*[49]). My point is not to split hairs over technology here. The technology has, in essence, leveled the playing field. While many people love talking about how great this is, what few people seem to be talking about is the reality that “newbies" are now expected to deliver products on par with seasoned professionals, regardless of genre and budget.

Shortcuts cannot be taken; excuses cannot be made. Either your short film will look and sound professional or it will not. This can be quite the monumental challenge for new filmmakers. For this reason, I highly recommend volunteering to be part of other productions. Observe and learn by personal investment in various roles necessary to make a short film. I also recommend looking through the appendices of this book for other books and resources

---

[46] *Like Crazy*, directed by Drake Dorms, 2011.

[47] *Act of Valor,* directed by Mike McCoy & Scott Waugh, 2012.

[48] *Prometheus*, directed by Ridley Scott, 2012.

[49] *Captain America: The Winter Soldier*, directed by Anthony Russo & Joe Russo, 2014.

filled with insightful information aimed at helping new filmmakers think through the many aspects of filmmaking that demand careful planning.

The reason I bring up quality first is because it is inevitably the first thing people will notice, consciously or subconsciously. There are so many other challenges that short films face that, for all practical purposes, making a low quality short film renders it invisible in today's online market. Viewers click on the next link before the film is over and forget ever having taken the time to look at even a portion of it in the first place. Naturally, that means they are not sharing the film in their social networks, which is how short films really get seen online. As a result, having a high standard of quality needs to be a foregone conclusion for filmmakers.

The Experiential Challenge

There is a profound and unaddressed divide that separates feature films from short films. I am convinced that, all things considered, audiences experience feature films and short films in fundamentally different ways. Because of this, comparing the experiences of watching short films to watching feature films tends to be an exercise in comparing apples and oranges. Where this really becomes a challenge for filmmakers is that audiences tend to expect from short films the same level of emotional catharsis that feature films are able to accomplish. As Linda J. Cowgill points out, "Short films are prone to anticlimaxes because the nature of the short form (from more limited budgets to less time for building the drama) requires a more subtle resolution than the long form drama."[50] Without realizing it, audiences tend to ask an awful lot of short films—possibly more than most short films are capable of delivering.

First of all, when we sit down to watch a feature film, most people still either attend a movie theater or sit down comfortably on their sofas at home and turn on their television sets. However, there is an increasing number of people who use their tablets and laptops, even their smart phones.[51] I suspect a larger amount of the content consumed on such devices tends to be episodic, not cinematic. Nevertheless, the viewing experiences that seem ideal to most filmmakers involve either screening a film in a theater or on a good television set at home during a mostly distraction-free time. For our purposes here, I will refer to these ideas jointly as "ideal viewing conditions" for a movie.

This, however, is not how short films are viewed today. Short films, for the most part, do not enjoy such an ideal viewing condition. Most short films are seen on computer screens, phones, and tablets. Experience of sound quality may vary dramatically as some viewers might wear good headphones and hear every whisper (and flaw) in the audio mix while others will simply watch the film using the tiny speakers on their tablet or laptop.

Why does this matter? I would like to suggest that this kind of

---

[50] *Writing Short Films: Structure and Content for Screenwriters* by Linda J. Cowgill, Watson-Guptill Publications, 2005. Page 133.

[51] The changes in viewing habits by moviegoers are on-going and we have yet to truly see how these changes affect the experience of each viewer. Ultimately, diving into a discussion about viewing feature films and episodic television shows on tablets and smartphones is outside of the scope of this book, though I suspect that any film viewing experience that allows for increased distraction (even watching a movie in the theater while texting) ultimately is detrimental to the intended experiential telos of the film.

experience of a movie is fundamentally different than what people have in mind when they think of watching a movie. It creates non-ideal viewing conditions that have subtle but important drawbacks on the viewing experience. There is a reason why the movie theater continues to be a valuable place for experiencing cinematic storytelling. For exactly this reason, most theaters now seek to preserve an ideal viewing condition by requesting that moviegoers refrain from using their cell phones for talking or texting during a film as this creates distractions and infringes on the ability of other moviegoers to experience the ideal, distraction-free viewing condition that they paid good money for in the first place.

There are even more profound philosophical reasons why all of this matters. Since it would take too many pages to go into all of these reasons and remain within the scope of this book, I highly recommend interested readers pick up a copy of Colin McGinn's thoroughly thought-out and incredibly engaging philosophical exploration of the cinematic experience in his book, *The Power of Movies: How Screen and Mind Interact.*[52] [53] Even though I cannot explain all of the ways in which non-ideal viewing conditions introduce drawbacks to the viewing experience, I would like to highlight a key difference in the viewing experience of most feature films compared to short films.

In a darkened theater or in the comfort of our own living rooms, there are generally long-established habits of movie-viewing. It is easy for us to sink into the experiential nature of

[52] *The Power of Movies: How Screen and Mind Interact* by Colin McGinn, Pantheon, 2005.

[53] I should point out that my appreciation for this particular book by McGinn does not in any way extend to his professional and personal behavior that led to his resignation from his teaching post at the University of Miami.

movies because this is what we do when we sit down on our sofa or in a movie theater seat. There is a pattern of letting go of other distractions (expect maybe popcorn, though even the popcorn might be an aid if we associate it with experiencing a movie) in order to open ourselves up to the movie experience before us. We know we are about to sit back and soak in a story for the next hour and a half to two hours. So, our minds settle in to the viewing experience in a way that is not likely to happen while sitting at our computers or watching something on our tablets to pass a few minutes.

In fact, I suspect that many short films viewed online are seen as a quick getaway from work and other demands on our time. Sitting at a computer, something most people these days are required to do in some capacity for work, strikes me as a truly terrible way to experience a film. After all, it can be hard for our ever-busy minds to let go, even momentarily, of the demands of work emails that need to be read and answered, or a friend's post on Facebook that beckons to us, or our home budget spreadsheets that need updating, or those items on Amazon that need to be purchased before it's too late; the list goes on. Likely, things are probably only worse on our smartphones and tablets.

This is the environment in which we are expected to release our short films today. It is a world of a million distractions and the constant drive to click or tap on the next thing, to scroll on after getting just enough information to leave a comment on Facebook or determine if something might be worth re-tweeting. The challenge that confronts filmmakers making short films today is one of daunting proportions. It is one thing to make a film with the expectation that those who opt-in to watching will sit-down and willingly immerse themselves in the experience of the film, but it is quite another challenge to make a film with the understanding that, at best, most people will only sort of watch it, their minds distractedly being pulled in a hundred other directions.[54]

This gets to a fundamental issue with storytelling. Consider these words from Lisa Cron taken from her book about the neuroscience of novel writing:

> Evolution dictated that the first job of any good story is to completely anesthetize the part of our brain that questions how it is creating such a compelling illusions of reality. After all, a good story doesn't feel like an illusion. What it feels like is life. Literally. A recent brain imaging study reported in Psychological Science reveals that the regions of the brain that process the sights, sounds, tastes, and movements of real life are activated when we're engrossed in a compelling narrative. ... When a story enthralls us, we are inside of it, feeling what the protagonist feels, experiencing it as if it were indeed happening to us, and the last thing we're focusing on is the mechanics of the thing.[55]

It seems that viewers of short films online are so often in non-ideal circumstances for movie watching that I am not convinced they are engrossed enough, as Cron says above, to trigger that kind of cognitive engagement in the narrative. I suspect that most

---

[54] It is precisely for this reason that most filmmakers passionately oppose the practice of some moviegoers pulling out their phones and texting or checking Facebook during a movie. The experiential-emotive nature of cinema is *only* at its peak when we as audience members willingly surrender all attention to it.

[55] *Wired for Story: The Writer's Guide to Using Brain Science to Hook Readers from the Very First Sentence* by Lisa Cron, Ten Speed Press, 2012. Page 4.

of the time, viewers watching short films tend to watch with one eye on the clock, too often thinking something along the lines of, "How soon will this be over so I can get back to what I was doing? What am going to eat tonight? Did I remember to pay that credit card bill? I should do that as soon as this ends. Is this thing going to get to the point already? I need to get back to work!" As filmmakers, our sincere efforts to tell a meaningful story may well be met with a "hurry up, already" attitude that could make even Michael Bay feel like he made a meandering Terrence Malick film.[56]

I have also heard it expressed before that with feature films, audiences need the first ten minutes of the film in order to simply forget about their day and settle into the experience of the movie. Once the audience is past those introductory ten minutes they are then able to turn off the analytical sides of their brains and engage in the primarily emotive experience of movies. No wonder audiences are in a hurry. Think about it, according to that theory, it takes up to ten minutes for our brains as viewers to become fully engaged in the narrative, or to move out of a state in which we might more readily focus merely on the mechanics of the storytelling.

The trouble is, in today's online environment, the demand is for incredibly short short films, or what I would call "micro-shorts" that range between one to five minutes. Even if your film is fifteen or twenty minutes long, that means most or half of your film is lost to that "settling in" period of time, assuming people hit play on the film in the first place. The reality is that longer short films do not seem to do as well online. Much like reluctant readers will check the page count in a book before starting, I

---

[56] For the record, Terrence Malick is my favorite director.

suspect online viewers check the running time of a short film before making the choice to hit play or not. I know I do and I love short films. I'm just busy. We all are!

Going back to our ten-minute theory as it pertains to feature films, once we, as viewers, are past those first several minutes, our minds adjust to the emotive experience of movies and we submerge our consciousness into the world of the story and the lives of the characters. A crucial element in storytelling is empathy. Empathy is how our brains latch onto the character and their stories and then, we experience it all as if we, ourselves, were in their shoes. Lisa Cron puts it this way:

A recent study, in which subjects underwent functional magnetic resonance imaging (fMRI) of the brain while reading a short story, revealed that the areas of the brain that lit up when they read about an activity were identical to those that light up when they actually experience it. ... In short, when we read a story, we really do slip into the protagonist's skin, feeling what she feels, experiencing what she experiences.[57]

This happens thanks to mirror neurons in our brains that allow us to empathize with characters and even feel like we're part of the action on-screen. Cron here is speaking of reading short stories. Imagine how much more this is the case with cinema, a primarily experiential medium as opposed to literature, which is primarily cognitive in nature.[58] Our brains are wired in such a way as to have dual neural pathways. One pathway is responsible for analytical and critical thinking. The other pathway is responsible for empathic thinking, where we set logic aside for

---

[57] *Wired for Story: The Writer's Guide to Using Brain Science to Hook Readers from the Very First Sentence* by Lisa Cron, Ten Speed Press, 2012. Page 67.

[58] Again, see *The Power of Movies* by McGinn for more on this.

the moment and think with our emotions, feeling what others feel or experiencing fully our own emotions.[59] According to the current understanding of our brains by neuroscience, these two pathways cannot be active at the same time, but their long-term effect is that we hopefully find balance between logic and emotion. The challenge for filmmakers is that cinema is designed to work on our empathic thinking.[60] Again, this is fine if audiences find themselves in ideal viewing conditions. However, when viewers engage short films in non-ideal conditions and also face the challenge of not having the time to sink into the experience of the story, like they might with a feature film, I believe viewers never turn off the neural pathways responsible for critical thinking. That means the neural pathways for empathic thinking are not turned on!

Because of this, I believe most viewers watch short films in such a fundamentally different state of mind that it can hardly be compared to the experience of viewing a feature film. And, in large part, this is probably why short films no longer follow a "mini-feature" structure and feel. It just doesn't work. Few viewers come along for the ride. Instead, viewers tend towards criticism and analysis in the moment rather than first experiencing. This amplifies any shortcomings of a short film, which is why I first started off discussing how important quality is to shorts today. I suspect that with some viewers, a highly negative response to short films is often due to an inability to empathetically immerse themselves into the story. They remain in critical mode and even possibly dispense harsher criticism than

---

[59] See Yo Yo Ma's article, "Behind the Cello." www.huffingtonpost.com/yoyo-ma/behind-the-cello_b_4603748.html?utm_hp_ref=tw

[60] Which is probably why there are plot holes in your favorite movie, but you just don't care.

a short film might have merited if they had been able to connect with the characters and their journey on an empathic level.

For all these reasons, short film viewing today is presented with significant challenge. Not everything is bad news, however. In the next chapter we will explore how we can respond to these challenges.

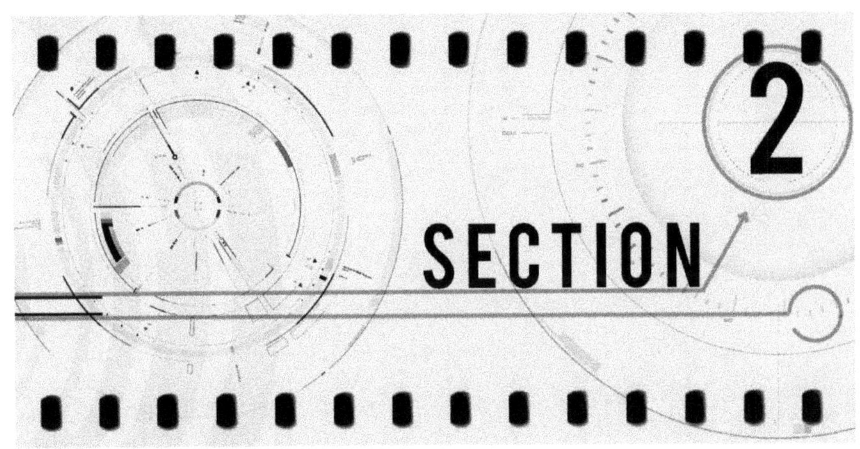

Making Short Films in the Digital Age

Embracing challenges as fuel for creativity.

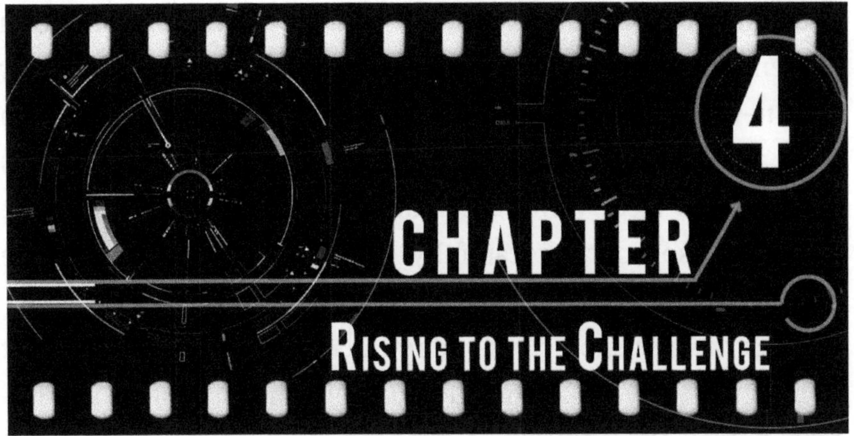

The challenges we face as creators of short films can appear quite daunting in light of what we have discussed in the last chapter. I hope the previous chapter was not too depressing. I do find that a healthy dose of reality can be sobering. Ultimately, out of such reality checks comes the ability to think creatively as we seek to actually address the challenges. That is my goal in this chapter. How shall we go about making better short films that overcome today's challenges? I would like to offer up several methods that I believe will collectively equip new filmmakers to dive into short film creation with increased effectiveness.

Watch Short Films

Being well versed in short films is a great place to start. Many new filmmakers I meet have spent an awful lot of time watching feature films. This is a fine thing, but as the previous chapters suggest, exposure only to feature film structures and plots are a very different thing compared to having an intimate awareness of how short films function today. Therefore, as a new filmmaker, watch as many short films as you can, especially now that Vimeo and YouTube provide a virtually endless stream of short film content for our viewing pleasure. There is really no excuse for why new filmmakers should not be *incredibly* well-watched in short films. In fact, try to make a point of watching short films both in non-ideal viewing conditions as well as ideal viewing conditions so you can carefully analyze for yourself how the experiences may differ for you.

Pick the best short films and rewatch them several times. Soak in both the story and techniques. Examine how the story is told - take notes! How quickly is the central problem of the plot introduced (chances are it happens within seconds)? What about the short film grabs your attention and how (does it start with conflict or immediately ask a question)? What shortcuts does the film take to quickly deliver exposition and context by relying on ideas commonly familiar to viewers? When in the short do important things happen? Your jottings will give you a sense of how various short films are paced and how they are structured to trigger our brain's natural inclination to find out what happens next, as Lisa Cron explains, any effective story does. Also write down things that maybe do not work in your opinion. Reflect on these problem areas and make notes as to why you think they do not seem to work.

Do not be afraid to watch bad short films. You can learn things from watching bad films as well as good ones. All of the above questions apply. You just might be exploring why a film does not work in order to better understand how to avoid similar pitfalls in your own projects. This can be valuable information to consider.

When possible, check out the filmmaker's website behind a particularly good film so you can see more of their work. In doing so, you might be able to note patterns of style, story subject, and even learn about the process undertaken to make a particular film.[61] Often times, if you have astute observations about a short film and questions about how it was written or made, filmmakers behind short films are quite happy to respond to comments on YouTube and Vimeo or even to respond to emails. I have answered many questions about my own projects on YouTube over the last few years.

Read Short Stories and Poetry

Back in Chapter One, I quoted Michael Rabiger. He pointed out that short films have far more in common with shorter forms of writing, such as poetry. With this in mind, I find it helpful to make the time to expose myself to good poetry and short stories. Poetry provides a different experience from the everyday through verbal expression of profound ideas, abstract thoughts, or simply capturing emotions in a unique way. And most poems are quite short. Many tell stories or provide a glimpse of an emotion or moment. I imagine good poetry reading works best when the empathic neural pathways are engaged. Stimulating your brain this way will not automatically make you a better filmmaker, but it might help you see how poets seek to build emotion and empathy or craft pictures in your mind. It also just might unleash all kinds of short film ideas.

Another literary medium worth exploring is the short story. Short stories face many of the same narrative limitations that

[61] When I released "Stop" online, I also released several short behind the scenes videos detailing various aspects of making the film, from writing to scoring the short. I got a lot of really positive feedback from people eager to learn all they could about the filmmaking process.

short films deal with. Novels, on the other hand, have the ability to take ample time to introduce characters and provide us with backstory and exposition and even atmosphere. There is plenty of space to engage in careful set-up and payoff within the plot. Novels also tend to have subplots that run through the narrative, mirroring or countering the main plot. But, short stories, especially the really short ones, often capture just a moment and have a limited perspective on a story. Reading really good short stories may help you see how literary writers have embraced and made the most of the confines of short story writing. The best short stories are incredibly focused in much the same way that the best short film plots are concentrated. While longer short stories still have the luxury of developing plot in a more leisurely pace than most short films, understanding how good writers effectively move a short story's plot forward is a helpful exercise. I find reading short stories helps ignite my imagination as I consider how to craft short films that drop audiences instantly into the middle of conflict. And of course, there are short short stories, or flash fiction, which are only a few hundred words and can share a lot of similarities with the structure of many five-minute short films given their remarkable brevity. Just as you might make notes about what works and what doesn't when watching a short film, it might be worth taking note of such things after reading a short story.

Embrace Brevity

In our highly individualistic culture where supposedly any of us can be anything we want and limits are supposedly meant to be shattered, the concept of embracing limitations can be quite counterintuitive. After all, the pervasive attitude would have us believe we should break through all limitations. However, true innovation first understands and embraces certain limits in quest to shatter others. Limitations are precisely what good short films are made of. Think about it: because we want to tell a story in ten minutes or less, we have a serious limitation on the amount of time we can take to tell our story. The best thing to do is to love that limitation and to find the most creative way to accomplish your goal within that construct. Rather than see these limits as annoying burdens, we need to see them as guidelines that help create a path to the best version of our story and give us a means to find our story's focus.

Another way to think of limitations is simply to view them as the rules of the game we are playing. The rules of basketball are such that no player is allowed to pick up the ball and simply run headlong into other players in an attempt to make it to the other end of the court, where they can then attempt to dunk the ball. I could argue that not being able to do so is placing a major limitation on my ability to play basketball, but you might correctly counter with the reality that, if I am allowed to break the rules of basketball in this way, I am no longer actually playing basketball in any meaningful sense of the word. If I am struggling to figure out a means to get to the other end of the court with the ball, in hopes of scoring, I am simply going to have to learn how to play the game within the limitations of the rules (or the guidelines) that make basketball, 'basketball'. In the same way, if we hope to make effective short films in the current online climate, we will need to play within the rules of today's game. Of course, where art differs from sports is that good artists first learn the rules then they figure out how to *effectively* break the rules.

And, when they do so, they are hailed as innovators, whereas athletes who break rules are viewed (rightfully so) as cheaters. The best artists know the rules long before breaking them, and generally break rules only selectively when it is the most effective means to tell a given story. Because of the fluid nature of art, the rules are subject to change, which is why short films have changed from mini-features to something more reminiscent of poetry or flash fiction.

Given the short running time expected of short films today, we might have to rethink a few things that might be deeply ingrained in our minds. One of the more recent difficult realizations I have come to is that opening credits really have no place in short films. While my 2011 short film, "Stop", had opening credits, I have since realized how little they add to the film and that—let's face it—nobody cares about them. The website, *Film Festival Secrets*, had a wonderful podcast episode on the top three mistakes short films make today, and forgoing opening credits and speeding up closing credits made the top three list![62] As much as I might be in love with the story I'm telling and as much as I'm feeling a profound emotional impact as the end credits roll, having drawn-out end credits can be a real buzz kill for a short film. For one thing, credits add to the total running time of a short film. When people see a video on YouTube, they see an eleven-minute short film and not a nine-minute short film with two minutes of end credits. And they ask themselves if they really have eleven whole minutes to give up at this moment. Nine is a single digit number. It can be easier for

---

[62] The episode titled "Top 3 Mistakes of Short Filmmaking" is no longer available on their website, though their site does indicate that the episode is available on iTunes podcast. Simply search for Film Festival Secrets Podcast.

someone to potentially think, "well, it's not even ten minutes long." But, eleven minutes is a whole ten minutes of their lives and then some—a big investment. And, of course, keep in mind that realistically, the ideal running time for short films is likely closer to five minutes and under. So now, if you have a four-minute short film with one minute of end credits, that means that a whole one-fifth of your film is the credits. That seems excessive!

Even if your concern is not with the movie's online reception, keep in mind that film festivals want to program as many short films as possible. So your two minutes of credits may take up time they would like to give to another film, or it may push the schedule too tight. I have actually experienced this as a festival judge and organizer myself where a film submission had painfully long credits. Thankfully, we were able to ask the filmmaker to provide us with a version of the film with shorter end credits so we could make our programming work and still include the film. For a lot of festivals, however, with hundreds of submissions each year, it is just easier to reject that film and program something else just as good with shorter credits. Do your film a big favor and don't draw things out with long opening and closing credits. That is most definitely the territory of feature films. Just get in, tell your story, and get out!

It's not enough to just have quick credits, though. There's a deeper philosophical approach that needs to be addressed as well. The reality is that new filmmakers need to shift their thinking away from making that "mini-feature" short film that runs 25 to 40 minutes. You are better off saving that type of storytelling for when you actually make a feature. Instead, set up the challenge for yourself to write and make a few short films that run between five and ten minutes in length. The very nature of such a quick story will require you to break out of the "mini-feature" plot structure. This will not only give your finished film a better shot at garnering a larger viewership and possibly getting into more festivals, it will likely also provide you with three other perks: a way to hook viewers quickly, a meaningful story, and a highly shootable script.

Writing such short scripts can be quite challenging, but rising to this challenge will make you a better storyteller. As Linda J. Cowgill points out in her book, *Writing Short Films*, "A good idea for a short film needs to be focused and specific. It doesn't have time to leisurely explore more than one topic."[63] She also notes that, "The best story ideas for short films are relatively simple. They can often be told in a single sentence."[64] I think she is correct about these things. I do feel it is important to note, however, that *Writing Short Films* by Cowgill was published in 2005. In other words, Cowgill approaches short films from a distinctly pre-YouTube perspective. In much of the book she uses twenty to thirty minute short films as her examples and addresses structural concerns related to writing scripts roughly thirty pages in length. In other words, Cowgill's book addresses the structural concerns of the "mini-feature." So, while there is plenty of sound advice in *Writing Short Films*, it has also been rapidly rendered out of date in regards to its perspective on appropriate short film length and structure. In fact, by reading Cowgill's book, it helped me realize the gap that exists in finding good books that address the unique challenges currently facing short films.

When writing a script that might be only five or six pages

---

[63] *Writing Short Films: Structure and Content for Screenwriters* by Linda J. Cowgill, Watson-Guptill Publications, 2005. Page 14.

[64] *Writing Short Films*, page 15.

long, the real discipline is in knowing how to pack in as much information as possible, within as few words as possible. I do appreciate Cowgill's admonition on this point when she says, "Good writers must learn to be good actors, too, so that they understand what must be said and what can go unsaid, and then figure out how to effectively communicate that on the page."[65]

Embracing brevity begins with the script. It can be incredibly tempting to design the film around showcasing some particular talent or new filmmaking gear. As long as the story really is served by these things, showcasing them is fine, but, too often, the story is not served by these devices or techniques. So, it is generally best to start with a solid script that succinctly engages in the central conflict of the story immediately. As Lisa Cron puts it when talking about the need for novels to hook readers, "A story must have the ability to engender a sense of urgency from the first sentence. Everything else—fabulous characters, great dialogue, vivid imagery, luscious language—is gravy."[66] The same is true of films (short or feature).

The temptation many new filmmakers face is to simply create some semblance of a story that allows them to imitate the styles of their favorite directors or cinematographers, thus, placing a higher value on style than story. But style for style's sake is artistic masturbation. Consider the following words of caution from influential screenwriting teacher, Robert McKee, "The aesthetics of film are the means to express the living content of story, but must never become an end in themselves."[67] Ultimately,

---

[65] *Writing Short Films*, page 8.

[66] *Wired for Story: The Writer's Guide to Using Brain Science to Hook Readers from the Very First Sentence* by Lisa Cron, Ten Speed Press, 2012. Page 21.

[67] *Story: Substance, Structure, Style, and the Principles of Screenwriting* by Robert McKee, Harper Entertainment, 1997. Page 26.

focusing on style over conflict is a sure-fire way to alienate audiences or simply fail to make them care about your characters and the story you are trying to tell.

There are also other practical advantages to making shorter short films. Making a five or six minute film is often something that can be done in one or two shooting days. Even a ten minute short film might be shootable in a single day or weekend, depending on how many locations, lighting changes, and camera set-ups are involved. This means that the expense of making such a film is minimal. You might even be able to enlist friends or other enthusiastic filmmakers who may be eager to work on more projects and build their résumé as volunteers. Just be sure to do a good job planning and preparing in pre-production so these shoots can be incredibly fun, quick, and inexpensive. By doing a project with this mentality, you can spend little on shooting the film and have money to use for either marketing, festival submissions, or other expensive post-production processes that might be required, should your film need visual effects or an elaborate score. It just depends on what goals you have for your film and what resources are at your disposal.

The second practical advantage to making such films is that you can quickly see a project from inception to completion. Being able to see a project through to the end is what separates the many wannabe filmmakers from those that actually make a go of things. You will also grow more quickly since, in a very short amount of time, you can gain experience in the three distinct areas of filmmaking: pre-production, production, and post-production. This kind of experience, even on a tiny project, is invaluable and will only make you more prepared for taking on more demanding projects in the future. By quickly finishing a small project, you may gain unexpected insights. For instance, what you thought was wonderful writing in your script may have turned out to be quite difficult to shoot, but you managed to shoot it anyway. Then you slugged through the editing process only to discover that the film was far more difficult to cut together than expected. The same elements that proved difficult to shoot probably also hurt the flow the editing. Seeing how audiences react to your finished project might help you see the whole story in a new light, bringing much needed insight into how to avoid such problems on the next project as you grow in your understanding of what audiences are actually connecting with.

Finally, the risk is minimized on micro-shorts. Consider the scenario from the previous paragraph: what if you find yourself in such a position and the film is essentially unsalvageable in editing? Well, the time and money you have invested in making such a project is hopefully minimal. If necessary, you can scrap the project with little tangible loss and chalk it up to being a very valuable learning experience, but hopefully that is truly a last resort. On the other hand, if you embark on making a larger short film project, say a thirty minute film with a budget of several thousand dollars, there will be no possible way you would want to scrap the project in post-production, even if you find that it is unsalvageable. Most likely, you will sink more time and money into rewriting and reshooting scenes to try to arrive at a passable finished product (and sadly its weaknesses will still likely show).[68] So, appreciating brevity in your early projects is a surefire way to ensure you don't end up in this series of stressful situations.

---

[68] Of course, if you are still determined to make a thirty-minute short film, I have to ask you, *why*???

EMBRACE WRITING... AND REWRITING... AND REWRITING...

You might be eager to produce every idea you come up with initially (or possibly simply fearful that the few ideas you might have at the moment are the only ones you'll ever have). This is an understandable impulse (and fear). However, I recommend taking some time to develop a few ideas. Write down quick descriptions of your ideas. Outline these ideas in detail. Then write the scripts. Even with a short film script in hand, carefully examine it before embarking on production. You may want to just get busy writing a few more scripts. I definitely have several short film scripts that never saw production (and never will). I am glad I wrote them. I'm also glad I never shot them.

As you work on your concepts for short films, be sure to focus your story on its core idea. Get rid of any and every thing that is not essential to the central conflict of the story. It will only add length and slow down the short film. Remember, with the new wave of short films today, there is no room for distractions and rabbit trails, so dive into your conflict right away and make sure every moment of the script is intimately connected to that conflict. In order to accomplish this, focus on your characters. Who are they? Discover the moment within your story that ultimately changes them or is sure to have a profound effect to them going forward. Then hone in on that moment and build your script around that.

To do this you will need to know your story's theme. If you can't figure out your story's theme, try to find a single word that most accurately describes it. In the case of my short film "Stop," I would say the theme is "obsession." Then try to come up with a short sentence that uses that word to describe the theme of your film. Again, for "Stop" I would say the theme is "obsession leads to self destruction."

Why is theme so important? According to Lisa Cron, "Theme often reveals your take on how an element of human nature—loyalty, suspicion, grit, love—defines human behavior. ... Knowing the theme of your story in advance helps, because it gives you a gauge by which to measure your characters' responses to the situations they find themselves in."[69]

Once you have a script written, the best thing to do is to ask people to read it. Hopefully these will be people who understand how to read a screenplay. This can be a bit of a challenge, especially if you have written a screenplay for a film that is light on dialogue. Good script reading is a learned skill where the reader has to interpret the script and direct the movie in their mind in order to actually grasp whether or not a script is all that good, or to be able to understand where its weaknesses might lie. And, of course, they have to do this on the fly as they read your script for the first time.

If you find you do not have people you can easily share the script with for good feedback, try sitting down with people and telling them the story, vividly, but briefly describing the visuals. See how people react. What kinds of questions are brought up? Do people point out flaws or holes in your story? Do several people point out that your short film seems rather similar to other movies already made? When first starting out as a storyteller, it is only natural to want to emulate our own favorite storytellers. I can personally attest to this and, for this reason, much of my early writing is not something that will ever see the light of day; you,

---

[69] *Wired for Story* by Cron, page 30.

too, may find that ultimately your first few short scripts are not something you actually want to produce. That is fine. Don't be discouraged. Just keep writing! Write as much as you can and, as you do produce some short films, hopefully your experiences in planning, shooting, and editing a short film will inform your writing in the future.

Never be afraid of revisions. I'm sure you've heard the old mantra before, "writing is rewriting." And it is quite true. Anne Lamott has a wonderful book about writing that I highly recommend.[70] My favorite chapter of the book is the crudely and appropriately titled, "Shitty First Drafts." Lamott lays out clearly that no matter how much we love that first draft, it's, well ... shit. Hopefully the bones are good, but so much still has to be fleshed out and polished and perfected. In the case of most of the short films I have written, I often express to people that I never stop revising; I just run out of time. The first day of shooting arrives, and I have to show up and direct something. I guess it better be the latest version of the script I've been poring over and the actors have been rehearsing. This is a bit of an exaggeration, but it's not that far from the truth on most of the films I have written and directed.

Finally, do not be discouraged if your early efforts in writing short films do not lead to great results. These things often take a lot of practice and only through practice do all of the various elements of good writing finally come together to offer up truly memorable stories. Along with writing a lot, I encourage you to read books about writing, such as *Story* by Robert McKee and others listed in the appendix. Few are those blessed with innate

---

[70] *Bird by Bird: Some Instructions of Writing and Life* by Anne Lamott, Anchor Books, 1995.

storytelling abilities. Okay, I'm being generous. No one has such skill innately! Most of us know a good story when we see it, but are hard pressed to write a good story without some much needed education and practice first.

Ira Glass addresses this beautifully in a video essay creative by David Shiyang Liu. He says that working in any creative medium involves an early awkward period of refinement where our skills as artists fall short of our ability to recognize good work by others. In other words, we may have great taste that inspires in us wonderful aspirations for creating excellent films, but our abilities to deliver on our own vision will fall short in those early days. Glass says he wishes someone had told him this long ago so he could have known that dealing with this gap between taste and skill is a necessary growth every artist faces. "Everybody goes through that," he says, "... and the most important possible thing you can do, is do a lot of work." The reason you should do a lot of work, Glass explains, is that only through such practice will you be able to finally close the gap between your taste and your ability. I find Ira Glass's honesty so encouraging that I suggest you take two minutes and watch the video right now.[71]

Embrace a Limited Budget

Let's face it; no one is going to give you millions of dollars to make a short film, or even hundreds of thousands of dollars, or probably even a thousand dollars. So, chances are that you will be making short films on very little money. Inevitably, the question of where to spend money will come up. The temptation for many

[71] "Ira Glass on Storytelling" by David Shiyang Liu, https://vimeo.com/24715531.

new filmmakers is to spend it on camera gear, and this is a natural temptation I have dealt with myself. The camera, after all, is this mysterious and amazing tool that is essentially advanced technology mixed with a little bit of magic, but the camera is not necessarily the most important expense on a short film (or any film, for that matter).[72]

As I've mentioned already, consumer-priced cameras are able to produce increasingly remarkable images (especially in the hands of skilled cinematographers), but the camera or lenses one decides to shoot with are an aesthetic choice. This should not be your first consideration when working on an incredibly tight budget for your short film. I have directed and shot projects for which I rented wonderful professional cine lenses.[73] The images for those projects are gorgeous! I have also directed and shot projects using much less expensive cameras and lenses. As someone who has been doing this for quite a while, I can tell the difference between the images, but even those projects shot on the "cheaper gear" still look wonderful (thanks to good gaffers and cinematographers). Ultimately, when I show these films, even projected on a large screen in HD, there's never been anyone in the audience that could tell we shot a given film with professional cine lenses that cost $7,000 each, as opposed to "prosumer" lenses that cost between $300 and $700 a piece.[74] The real question is, ultimately, how good was the storytelling?

---

[72] Just to be clear, I don't literally mean magic. I mean, when things click together on set, a camera can capture something so beautiful or true that it can never quite be reproduced again, but this wonderful piece of technology allows us to capture and preserve it and even give things a life all their own.

[73] Zeiss Super Speeds, Mark II, in case you were curious.

[74] Such as the inexpensive Rokinon "cine lenses" I own, which are really SLR lenses re-engineered to work more-or-less like actual cine lenses.

To this end, I believe in spending money in areas that truly affect the storytelling. In my most recent short film projects I have abandoned the notion of renting cameras and lenses. I own and know people who own adequate equipment to do the job on such projects. I am much more inclined at this point to spend money on production design, as this is something that will be clearly seen on screen and will have a direct impact on the audience's experience of the world in which the story is taking place (and whether or not they believe such a world and characters might exist). So, while I would love to shoot a short film on the latest, newest, and hottest camera to hit the market, I'll happily shoot it on what is already available to me, if my choice is between spending money renting or buying a camera and spending money making my set look truly like the world the characters within my script would inhabit. Of course, this is a choice I have arrived at for my own reasons and others are free to disagree, but I must strongly caution against the temptation to simply pour your entire budget into camera gear. The vast majority of the time, this will be a mistake.

There are other areas that you might want to consider spending money, such as making sure you capture good audio (we'll talk more about the importance of good audio in just a bit) or having someone create visual effects shots crucial for telling your story. In the case of my short film, "Parallel," I made sure to spend what little money we had available in having a friend, Chaz Sutherland, build an amazing prop that served as the window into another universe around which the whole story is centered. If the prop had not worked, if it had not been believable, if it had not merged so beautifully with the VFX by Shahnam Haider in the finished film, then the movie would not have worked. We shot it on cheaper lenses to invest in props. However, the work of my cinematographer Rajah Samaroo, gaffer Chris Tremblay, and colorist Stephen Webb ensured that the visual quality of the film is quite remarkable (and arguably better than the films I made with far more expensive lenses). You might find that your specific project may truly need more expensive camera gear. The point is to be sure to sit down during pre-production and carefully examine your script. Be brutally honest with yourself about what really is a priority when making your film. Don't sacrifice an area that will affect the story just to get the enjoyment or bragging rights of having gotten to shoot a project on the latest camera on the market (which will likely be old news by the time you finish your film anyway).

Embrace the Shot List

Your shot list really is something that is essential no matter the length of your film. Having a polished script may feel like enough preparation to go shoot your short film. Unfortunately, it really is not. You need a shot list. A shot list is exactly what it sounds like: a list of what shots you need to set-up and capture in order to have the appropriate raw footage so that you can actually cut the film together in editing. It is indispensable on the vast majority of projects (features, shorts, commercials, and even documentaries).

Think of it as your grocery list. However, there is a catch: you only have a very limited amount of time to get all your shopping done. Whatever has not been crammed into your shopping cart when that timer runs out are items that you will not be allowed to purchase, and you need to buy a lot of food. So, you must know exactly what you need to buy and where it is located in the store so that you can proceed to shop in as logical and efficient a manner as possible. There is no time for standing around staring at shelves of pasta trying to decide if you feel like making spaghetti or linguini. That was a decision that should have been made at home!

Filmmaking works much the same way. You will always have a limited amount of time to shoot projects, but on a short film it is often only a day or two. You have to account for all kinds of environmental factors like:

- When will the sun rise and set that day?
- What is the weather like?
- When and where will you eat lunch?
- Where will people go to the bathroom?
- Will there be electrical power?
- Is there enough room for all your gear?
- Will the location be locked down and completely yours or will there be random people walking through your set and disrupting things?
- Do you have permission to be there in the first place?

All of these and other factors are going to affect how you can accomplish shooting.

You will also need to plan ahead for any difficult shots, such as a complicated camera move that simultaneously involves performances from multiple actors that all has to happen in perfect synchronization. To be sure you have captured what shots you need, it will take a lot of time to set-up, rehearse, and then shoot enough takes. Even simpler scenes to shoot do not simply happen without significant forethought. At this point in my filmmaking career, I actually write a list of what needs to be shot before creating a shooting schedule to help me carefully plan how the day will flow and how best to organize the actors, lighting setups, etc. Planning is an essential part of filmmaking and, to accomplish all of this planning; you need to know what you are actually going to shoot. You need a shot list and shooting schedule!

What goes into a shot list is really a matter of thinking about the edit of the film. I realize that to new filmmakers, this can be a serious challenge. There's a bit of a catch here: if you have never edited a film before, how are you supposed to know what shots you need in the edit? It can be easy to simply shrug off a shot list and try to "just make it happen." Please allow me to share with you two diametrically opposed real experiences I had on two different sets.

First, I once was involved with a project by a very green director who never made a shot list. Everyday we would show up to set with no real plan other than knowing what scene or scenes we were going to try to shoot that day. The first two hours or so of our shooting day were regularly lost to the director standing around and staring at things on set, thinking about how to shoot the scene. At times, we did some blocking with the actors, which was followed by more standing around. Finally, he would have an idea of where to start shooting the scene and we would at last begin shooting. But, as we proceeded, he would invent more and more shots. Even though I was rather green myself, I had studied filmmaking at the LAFSC by this point and cut several of my own early short films. I knew enough to know that many of the shots this director was coming up with on the fly where not shots any sensible editor would ever use when cutting the film together: they would not fit with the flow of the scene; they would create awkward jumps in perspective; they would likely create an inconsistent visual style. On top of this, many of the shots he invented on the go overlapped material that we had already covered in two or three or four other angles.

Any sensible director or cinematographer is always thinking about how a scene will ultimately cut together and make camera placement and shot decisions based on how they envision the edit playing out and how they are utilizing the visual grammar (shot size, angle, movement, composition, lighting, color, so forth) of the particular style they have embraced for a given project. The problem was that this green director was his own cinematographer and his own editor. The concept of visual grammar was not even remotely on his radar, as the end product ultimately demonstrated. And, in spite of my warnings that he would likely never use certain angles in the final edit that he wanted to get on set, we spent a lot of time covering scenes with more camera set-ups than most Hollywood studio movies. This resulted in an incredibly slow and draining shooting pace on set that just drug on. And the real kicker? We were shooting a feature film! It's one thing to pull this kind of amateur stunt on your first short film over a grueling weekend. People are likely to forgive this and extend some grace to a first time filmmaker shooting his or her first short film. It is quite another matter to try to direct in this fashion on a feature film project. The patience of your cast and crew will run out long before you complete production.[75]

---

[75] This director had other very good qualities, but his lack of experience coupled with a stubborn determination to just keep doing things his way (which mostly meant him insisting on doing nearly every job on set himself) ultimately wore me out. I made the incredibly difficult decision to walk away from any

In spite of this director's lack of editing experience, it would still have been incredibly beneficial for him to at least think through each scene and try to compare it to other movies that he felt were similar to the one he was making. If you find yourself having a hard time making a shot list, I recommend the follow exercise:

1. Choose two or three scenes from major movies by seasoned directors. Be sure they are movies or scenes that are similar to the scene you are about to shoot.
2. Carefully watch the scenes a few times, making notes about the size of the frame, shot composition, and camera placement.
3. Note how the scene progresses. Does it start with a wide shot then cut into mediums or close-ups? Does it start on a close-up and cut to a wide in order to first introduce a character and then reveal their whereabouts? Does it use an establishing shot?
4. Note if the camera moves, is hand-held, or stationary. Does the camera pan or tilt to follow the action on screen?

By analyzing scenes that are similar to yours, you will be able to develop an understanding of how seasoned directors might approach shooting analogous material. Initially, such analysis can provide you with at least a rough template to follow. But, as you work through this process a few times, you will begin to grasp why directors make certain choices and why you might want to make

---

involvement with the project, but this experience has taught me so much about the importance of preparation and working with a good team. It has also given me a pretty good hack detector.

similar or different ones depending on the nature of your film project.

I wish the above director had engaged in this kind of preparation since he felt unable to create a shot list ahead of time. More importantly, he might have managed to grasp the nature of style and visual grammar and made better choices about how to cover each scene. He might have grasped how movement, low angle shots, high angle shots, composition choices, frame size, and other cinema grammar elements could be best used to tell his story. His problem wasn't so much that he lacked knowledge as much as he was in too much of a hurry to become an indie filmmaker making feature films. He should have taken the time to read good books on filmmaking and make several short films first, in order to develop firsthand knowledge of style and visual grammar before taking on a feature film. His haste led to him being ill-prepared to make a feature film and this was only compounded by his continued unwillingness to even try to plan ahead with a basic shot list. In the end, we lost countless hours on set and it hurt the final film significantly.

Once shooting wrapped, I am sure he spent far too long trudging through footage on his computer only to realize that cutting to certain shots was just not an option. In other words, such footage was ultimately shot for no reason. This wouldn't be of major significance, as it's common to shoot some footage that doesn't make the final cut, but when contemplating limited budgets on indie films, frugality should lead us to want to minimize such wastefulness. Even a small amount of footage deleted from the final cut of a film represents many hours of hard work by many people on set. Cutting more than just a small amount of footage from a feature film can easily represent whole days of production that simply did not need to have happened—exactly the opposite of responsible frugality.

In this particular case, the lack of a shot list also had another detrimental effect on the film. Having finally seen the finished film, I can honestly say that while it is a generally good-looking film, it lacks any sense of visual unity in terms of style or consistent and purposeful use of cinematic grammar to tell its story.

It is because of experiences like this that I wish everyone who aspires to become a director were required to shoot several short films on Super8 film first. The cartridges of film lasted only about three minutes and they cost a good bit of money to buy and have processed. At the LAFSC, we got only two or three cartridges for a project. We definitely could not shoot just any old thing that popped into our heads. If we did, we would run out of film stock and not have the footage to cut together for a project to turn in. We learned to plan quickly! But, the problem with many new directors in the digital age is that they often want to shoot anything and everything and then, simply sit down and actually make the movie in editing. I suspect many such directors don't like the tedious work of planning in pre-production. Others may be paralyzed by a fear of making a bad decision and feel safer having every conceivable option for the edit. In the case of the latter, I would simply point out that such a fear is actually a fear of directing. Directing involves making countless decisions. Someone with a fear of making decisions is in the wrong line of work if they are trying to become a director. In the case of the former, directors who don't feel like planning ahead are just plain lazy. Sadly, lack of planning generally makes a film set a frustrating and tense place to work for everyone involved. Such directors who choose not to plan do so at the expense of effective communication and smooth shooting.

As for the second story, which was more recent, I was the producer and cinematographer on a short film by a first-time director. This director struggled to compose a shot list. It is a challenging thing to think through initially. But, as his cinematographer, I happily sat down with him in advance and we talked through each scene of the short script. We talked about preferred shooting styles and aesthetic choices. Based on all of this, together we wrote down a shot list. I could tell it was a challenge for the director to wrap his mind around how to really think through the shots he wanted, but he stuck with it!

On the first day of shooting, we hit a few snags, but quickly recovered as we could look at our shot list and realize what needed to be adjusted or what no longer worked in light of things that had come up on set or blocking changes that were made in the moment. The point is, we had a plan that eliminated guesswork on set, but we were not locked into this plan without any flexibility or ability to revise the plan on the spot. Having a plan ahead of time does not kill creativity (something the director in the first story above never grasped)! It actually sets creativity free.

At the end of the first day of shooting, the director and I sat down to talk about what needed to happen on the second day. It was like a bright light bulb had come on in the director's mind. He smiled, his eyes filled with anticipation. "I get it now," he told me. "I understand the shot list now and I know what we need to do to make tomorrow's shot list!" We sat about making the shot list for the next day's scenes. It took us very little time! One day of shooting and this director knew what to do and understood the value and importance of the shot list.

I share these two stories to illustrate the options before you, even if you are totally new to filmmaking. With a short film, you can take the attitude of the first director and probably get away with it, but don't be surprised if people walk off your set if you try that on a feature—and rightfully so. Also, if you take the path of the first director, your short film will not be as good as it could be and you will likely end up realizing that you should have planned better. I believe that even if the concept of a shot list seems completely foreign to you, the only way to learn a foreign language is to immerse yourself in it. Ignoring it will not get you anywhere in the long run.

To make the best shot list, work with other experienced individuals and make use of technology. Working with other experienced individuals will only make you a stronger director, so seek out an experienced cinematographer who understands visual grammar, work with an assistant director who understands how best to schedule a shooting day, and consult with a seasoned editor who might be able to point out gaps or other problems in your shot list. Make use of the many tools available for smartphones and tablets today that help with the shot listing and storyboarding process, if you feel your project needs it—which some definitely do. In Appendix B, you will find a list of helpful apps, including my favorite, Shot Lister, which helps with planning a shoot and keeping it on schedule with live progress tracking. But, the only way you can use Shot Lister is to actually have a shot list.

Ultimately, planning is not the enemy of creativity. If you can learn to enjoy preparing, you will allow yourself the most creative options within your budget and experience. Having a plan of attack will allow you to make efficient use of time and resources on set and it will help ensure that you are happy with the footage you shot when you are sitting at your computer starting the editing process. Here is a mantra that I wish more indie filmmakers embraced: “Planning is not optional!”

Embrace High Standards

As I have already mentioned, audience expectations today take professional production quality for granted. This is why it is all the more important to gain hands-on experience with film projects before taking on a directing role. It also means that collaborating with other people who may be more experienced than you in filmmaking, especially the technical crafts, is essential these days. Bringing on talented crewmembers to your project will only help things run more smoothly. You will also have the benefit of being able to learn directly from these skilled crewmembers.

One quick word about embracing high standards: in this short book I will only be able to highlight some key areas. But, if you are serious about learning more about the filmmaking process, you will find a list of helpful books in Appendix A, as well as websites in Appendix C that discuss and teach various aspects of the evolving landscape of digital filmmaking. It is a moving target so there is always more to learn, even if you’ve been at it for years.

Once you have a polished script that you feel is ready for production, you may want to find someone with experience as a producer who might be willing to help you take on the task of bringing this project to fruition. If you cannot find anyone to produce with you, do not worry. On a first or second short film especially, it is not uncommon to need to go it alone as a producer/director. Chances are you know other people who would be excited to jump in and help bring a project to life. In Chapter Five, I will go into detail about the key areas that, in my experience, make someone a good producer. It will serve as a good jumping-off point, as you look for a good producer or equip yourself to be your own producer.

After finding your producer, you will want to make sure you find a good cinematographer. I have worked with many cinematographers and it always amazes me how important the relationship between cinematographer and director is to the finished film. So, do not simply look for the best technical or aesthetic sensibilities out there (though these are of incredible importance), but also look for kinship in stylistic preferences and approaches to storytelling. Naturally, developing your sense for this may take a while. Therefore, if you are making several projects, do not be afraid to try working with several cinematographers.

I have learned over time that two things really matter to me when it comes to cinematography. First, I need to feel like I have a good creative and collaborative working relationship with my cinematographer.[76] As Sidney Lumet put it, you want to make sure you are both making the same movie.[77]

The second characteristic I look for in a cinematographer is something that I have developed slowly over the years: find someone who knows as much or more than you do about

---

[76] I feel the same way when I am the cinematographer working for a director. A good collaborative and creative relationship is what will produce the best results. Being on the same stylistic page and having the same goal of telling the same story are crucial.

[77] See Lumet's *Making Movies*, Vintage Book, 1996.

cinematography. I am a cinematographer myself and know quite a bit about the science and technical aspects of shooting that is gained by continued reading and years of shooting experience on a wide variety of projects (from commercial work to highly stylized narrative projects). So when I'm directing, I look for a cinematographer who I feel knows as much or more about the science and technology of cameras and lighting as I do. Preferably, they know more and I get to learn more by working with them. I learn something new every time I direct!

Next, find a good audio mixer to record sound on set during shooting. Audiences will tolerate a grainy or low quality image, even embracing it as a stylistic choice by the director and cinematographer. But there is no grace for bad audio. When a film sounds bad, it looks bad too (no matter what it was shot on). Audiences are accustomed to Hollywood sound quality, which is very present dialogue that is clean and crisp and unencumbered by background noise. Background noise that changes suddenly every time the movie cuts to a new shot or interferences, static, and audio recorded from a microphone across the room so that it sounds like a home video—these are all surefire ways to ensure that your audience is distracted or doesn't take your film seriously.

Audio is one of the most under-appreciated aspects of filmmaking, probably due to the fact that truly great audio is invisible. You will never notice it unless you are actively listening for it and you know what to listen for, but the effect of good audio is very powerful on audience perception and emotional response to a film. This is why recording good sound on set is so important. Audio is difficult to clean up after the fact. If the microphone was not positioned correctly and it picked up far too much echo in a large room, the voices will not sound present and clean. In many cases, it can be impossible to clean up such audio, at which point you have to endure the headache of ADR (Additional Dialogue Recording or Automatic Dialogue Replacement, depending on who you ask). It is better to simply invest the time in getting the best possible audio on set, which will make the mixing process that much smoother.

The sound mix is another important and under-appreciated aspect of filmmaking. Often I watch short films where I notice a poor mix: obvious cuts in the audio, digital pops, abrupt changes in environment sounds, abrupt music stops, inconsistent dialogue levels between characters, or even audio that bounces between the left and right speakers without explanation. These and many other issues are all things a good sound mixer knows how to handle. In my early days as a filmmaker, I did all of my own audio mixing. Through this process, I learned the value of setting up a good environment for mixing. I have mixed in a recording studio with professional monitors and I have mixed on a high quality consumer surround sound system. In both scenarios, I managed to get great results.

The first real key to great mixing is painstaking attention to detail. Even subtle changes in audio can be distracting. By mixing my own films, I learned a lot about paying attention to the subtle quality changes in the audio and about how to match audio effectively to create a sense of unity in the soundtrack.

The second key is taking the mixed film out of the mixing environment and actually hearing it in various settings through all kinds of speakers. This is an old practice from music producers. After a while, your ears become quite accustomed to the speakers you happen to be using for your mix. And, if those speakers are high quality studio monitors, you may be given an ideal representation of your mix, which is the idea. But, what happens when someone hears your movie on tiny laptop speakers? Will that moment in the movie where the low bass in the score comes in softly even register? How does this change the viewer's experience and emotional response? You can find out if you go listen to the film on a laptop, then a TV, then an iPad, then some low-grade surround sound system, consumer headphones, and so forth. Only this way will you get a real sense of what people will hear as they watch your film in all kinds of settings.

Finally, the editor of a movie is one who wields great power over the finished film. Great writing, acting, directing, and cinematography can all be rendered moot if a film is poorly edited. Poor choices by an editor can make a great script seem mediocre or it can make a wonderful performance feel flat and lifeless. On the other hand, a great editor can rescue a film from derailing when you discover you just don't have what you need or there are problems with the footage, performances, or audio. Even problems with the script can sometimes be addressed. As I mentioned already, I served as the polishing editor of a feature film where my primary role was to creatively cut the film, so as to strengthen the pacing and story, by getting rid of everything that slowed it down or was unnecessary.

As a director, you have two options when it comes to editing a short film. You can work with an editor or you can opt to cut it yourself. With short films, it really depends on your goals. When I first started making short films, I was always my own editor. Sometimes I shared editing duties with my co-writer and fellow producer, Andrew Gilbert. Being my own editor taught me so much about how to really make a film, specifically the importance of coming up with a good shot list of angles that I was actually going to use in cutting the film and not just shots that sounded cool in my head or on the spot when shooting. This experience has proved invaluable in my development as a director and writer.

I also find that it's great to work with an editor. Having someone else cut your film is a great exercise in communication. Just as you might pick a cinematographer, based on his or her style and technical expertise, you can do the same when selecting an editor. I have worked with a few different editors and they have been great experiences. Each editor I have worked with has a unique perspective and strength. With this in mind, when contemplating a particular project, I can make a choice about who might be the best fit for the particular story and the particular style of film I am seeking to make.

However you chose to proceed, know that a film needs to go through various drafts—it needs to be polished, just like a script. Do not be afraid to show your work in progress and invite feedback from astute people you may know. Try to identify where the film is struggling and how you can address it. You should know that short films, especially early projects, often need to undergo many cuts (or drafts) before they are ready to be called a final cut. On the other hand, give yourself a deadline. It can be too easy for short film projects to languish in post-production, as I'll talk more about later. After all, short films are generally what new filmmakers manage to do in their free time between school and work and, without a deadline; it can be easy to fall into the trap of endlessly editing and polishing the film. If a particular project is presenting insurmountable challenges, I recommend simply finishing the film as best you can. You don't have to release it, but seeing it through to the end will teach you a lot. Once you are finished, you will be ready to take on the next project, except now, you will know firsthand the specific problems to avoid.

Embrace Good Casting

Casting your short film can certainly be a major challenge, but social media increasingly allows for great networking opportunities and there are a lot of aspiring actors out there. Many are quite talented. The important thing to keep in mind about casting is that ultimately audiences connect with characters and it is the actors who bring those characters to life. You could do everything else impeccably, but bad acting can so thoroughly derail a film that everything else might be forgotten by the audience. So, you should definitely spend the time to seek out good actors. Get involved with local theater and film groups. Hold auditions for your project and announce it through these groups and through social media. Even if you are making a small project with no money, you will be surprised by the number of talented actors looking for resume material. If you are going to submit your film to festivals and get it listed on the Internet Movie Database (IMDb), this can be a very worthwhile incentive for a lot of actors needing more material for their demo reel or looking to build their IMDb profiles. And yes, you should most definitely allow them to use material from your film on their reel.

Keep in mind that directing actors is a fine art that takes some development as well. Careful, open, and thoughtful communication is the only way to really direct performances. Giving line readings is not directing! Telling an actress that you merely want her to play a scene “more angrily” is not directing! Any experienced and sensible actors will be insulted by kind of shoddy directing. Real directing means communicating motivations out of your intimate connection to the journey the characters are on and the substance of the script. I cannot cover all that goes into good directing here, but I highly recommend two books by Judith Weston: *Directing Actors* and *The Film Director's Intuition*. As you work with actors, view them as fellow collaborators, not as mere marionettes to be manipulated (which is what giving line readings reduces them to). If you have done your job well in casting the film, trust your actors to discover the characters and bring them to life.

Embrace Substance

Having something unique and worthwhile to express through your story may be the most challenging aspect of making a great short film, but it is so important! You may have done all of the above things well, but if your story is about nothing, no one will ultimately care.[78] I see this far too often today in VFX-driven short films on the Internet. They are visually wonderful and they certainly showcase the talents of the director and VFX artists (frequently the same person on small projects). But, far too often there is no substance to the story; nothing of significance is communicated. To quote Robert McKee:

> The writer shapes story around a perception of what's worth living for, what's worth dying for, what's foolish to pursue, the meaning of justice, truth—the essential values.

[78] I recognize I am starting to sound like a broken record every time I say that you may have done everything else well but something else may yet derail your film. However, this is the cumulative nature of filmmaking and this is why it is so challenging to make truly great films.

> ... First we must dig deeply into life to uncover new insights, new refinements of value and meaning, then create a story vehicle that expresses our interpretation to an increasingly agnostic world. No small task.[79]

In an age where we are inundated with media, much of which is incredibly superfluous, it can be so hard to stand out from the noise of pop culture. But please allow me to present you with this challenge: dare to say something meaningful! Even if it makes you feel exposed and vulnerable, dare to wrestle with life through stories. This may seem like a massive accomplishment in a short film, but do not be intimidated. Remember the two examples we have been looking at over the course of this book, "Tune for Two" and "Cargo." These films are incredibly short. Yet they manage to say something worthwhile in their short running times. "Tune for Two" captures a darkly funny moment, but ends with a return to the status quo, which means a man is dead. But, for a few fleeting moments, these two men were not so different, connected by something so childish and catchy. Certainly this moment will haunt the hit man.

"Cargo" boils down parenting to its most elemental principal: ensuring the survival of your child. Thoughtful viewers might even find it worth discussing the concept of ensuring your child's survival against your own potential transformation into something horrible (a classic aspect of the zombie genre which consistently asks us who the real monsters are). Or, viewers might contemplate the reality of the risk of parenting, which means ultimately relinquishing your control and ability to protect your child in what can seem like a horrible and dangerous world. When

---

[79] *Story* by McKee, page 17.

the father rigs up his contraption to ensure that his zombie self will keep going and stay away from his daughter, he has no guarantee that his daughter will find safety or that other zombies will not happen upon them and kill her, but he does what he can in what little time he has left.[80]

I hope you see the point I am making. Neither of these films tries to explain in any way their "point." In fact, no good art tries to explain its "point." That is not good art, that's propaganda. Good art invites interaction, interpretation, and reflection.

When I came up with the concept for my short film, "Parallel," I was simply driving home one night and was struck by an interesting way to encapsulate the beautiful, fragile, and ultimately temporary nature of human relationships in this life. The whole story for "Parallel" simply flooded my brain in an instant. It was such a massive concept to try to make a ten-minute film out of the idea that I found myself incapable of actually writing it for a couple of weeks, even though the whole story existed in my mind already and needed no real outline. Finally, I mustered up the courage to write it down and see if all the swirling emotions and concepts in my head could make sense on the page. It was a rather significant personal risk in terms of making me vulnerable, given how visceral my reaction was to the idea. I honestly couldn't write the story for days, after it first occurred to me, because I felt sure I might be reduced to a sobbing heap on the floor. Finally, as the raw power of the emotions settled I was able to write. As I showed people the script, reactions were universally positive and I knew I needed to make

[80] As a father of a beautiful little girl myself, I cannot keep from bursting into tears no matter how many times I've seen this short film as I contemplate all of my own realities and responsibilities of being her father.

the film in spite of my own fears that it might be too ambitious of a story, but that is the most exhilarating type of risk to take as a storyteller!

What haunts you, bothers you, breaks your heart, brings you joy, gives you hope? These are your stories to tell. If you are willing to look inside your soul and ask potentially frightening and sobering questions of yourself, there are truly great stories to be birthed from within you—stories the world needs to hear. Don't just make a short film; bring a little hope and beauty into this world!

The one thing that truly stands between most filmmakers and making a successful project is the ability to plan (or lack thereof). We have touched on this already in our discussion about the importance of having a shot list, but planning out your short film is much more than a shot list. There is a different area of planning, of true logistical execution that reaches far beyond a shot list. I'm talking about producing... really producing!

For new filmmakers, thinking like a producer can be incredibly hard unless they are already administratively gifted. Great producing can be incredibly unglamorous, but great producing makes all the difference in the world when you and your crew are standing on set and a fuse is blown or lunch is late or unexpected rain drops begin to plummet from the sky. Great producers have thought ahead to these scenarios and considered how to address these situations. Producers are, in essence, the operational, logistical, and financial managers of the film world.

If you are making short films, chances are you will need to function both as director and as producer. In fact, I encourage this. I think everyone who wants to direct needs to produce their own early projects, even if it is in conjunction with another producer. That is not to say everyone should go it alone, but I do sincerely believe that every aspiring director needs to have a very thorough understanding of what a producer does, especially in this age of increasingly minimal budgets, even for feature films. Knowing how to think like a producer (and in many regards, like an assistant director) means that, as a director, you will be better equipped to make savvy, frugal decisions about where to save time and money. This will empower you creatively, as it will free up that time and money for other areas that might truly need extra attention or resources. Directors who refuse to understand the realities of producing are like a runner who believes she can win a marathon without training. So let's talk about some basics of efficient and effective producing.

Valuing People

People make movies—specifically, groups of people and often large groups of people. Filmmaking is not a medium for anyone seeking to work in solitude, like a novelist or painter who has complete control over every word on every page or every brushstroke on each canvas. This is a collaborative medium that takes into account the talents and skills of many diverse personalities and it can seem like, at times, it takes the populous of a small country to make it all happen. Sure, there is a guiding artistic vision that ultimately sets the tone and direction for a film production and this is found in the role of director, but good directors are collaborators at heart; as are producers.

With this in mind, I find that it is very helpful to start any discussion about producing by talking about something that might seem rather obvious: working with people. Great producers understand the realities of working with a crew of diverse personalities where each department is focused on doing their very best work even as the producer and assistant director seek to keep the production moving forward with swiftness and efficiency. Sadly, I have encountered too many situations in which producers have not thought carefully about the logistics of working with people.

When planning a production, a good producer (and production manager) will always think about all of the logistical considerations that are easy to forget when simply watching a finished film. There is a crew and cast of several people with requirements and requests to be considered. The cast is going to need a place to change into their wardrobe, to have makeup applied, and possibly to run lines or simply step away from the franticness of work on set so they can concentrate and prepare for their performance. Meanwhile your crew will need a place to wait between set-ups. You will need a place to serve snacks and food to everyone. Everyone showing up to set that day will need to park and everyone will need restrooms. At times, a producer may even need to play the role of conflict manager to help quell any personality clashes or other social issues that may arise from working with a diverse group of people.

Forgive me if this might seem obvious to you and I. There is an old saying that “if common sense were common, more people would have it”, and unfortunately, this is the case for many out there making movies today. Allow me to tell you a story, but, before I tell you, I have to warn you that the following story may sound downright unbelievable. Yes, it really happened!

I was once hired to assistant direct a short film project with an emotionally compelling script. Like many short film projects, it had a very limited budget. So I volunteered my time, as did nearly everyone else on the project. In the end, they did give me a little money to cover some of my gas expenses in driving to and from set, for which I was grateful. During shooting, however, it became clear to me that some basic logistics had not been considered in advance. This became painfully clear one day on set when we were shooting a scene in a residential area.

It was winter in New England and on this particular day the temperature outside was only barely above single digits. Our crew had no shelter from the cold. We were expected to bundle up and deal with the cold for hours on end. As if that wasn't enough, this particular producer was so paranoid about being sued, should someone on the crew spill a hot drink on themselves, that she did not provide the crew with hot coffee, hot chocolate, or tea as a means to help at least alleviate the effects of the cold. We were free to go spend our own money (on this unpaid gig) if we wanted to get something hot to drink, but the trouble with deciding to drink anything that day was the fact that we had no bathrooms on set. We did not have the permission from any of the local residents to use their guest bathroom while shooting in the neighborhood. The best we could do was hope for a break in shooting, run back to our cars parked a block or two away from set, drive to a local convenience store several blocks away, and ask to use their bathroom.

As if all of this still wasn't bad enough, at one point on this particularly cold day, the lead actor of the short film—who also happened to be an executive producer on the project—decided he needed another thirty or forty minutes of time to sit in his comfortably warm car and meditate in order to prepare himself for his performance (which was only a matter of pulling up to a house in his car—I kid you not). Given that he was an executive producer and the producer was on his side, even though I was the AD, I had no authority to simply say that this was unacceptable and force shooting to proceed. In the end, I stood with my crew in eleven-degree weather while we waited for our lead actor to make himself "ready to shoot." That was when I realized I would never work with that producer and EP ever again. Their priorities were made clear that day. The wellbeing of their crew had never crossed their minds.

This is the frame of mind I am coming from when I say that these logistical considerations are of fundamental importance. In the case of that short film, it had a clear adverse effect on the morale of the whole crew. Eventually, we all felt devalued and unappreciated. We did our best to maintain a professional demeanor, but I have no shame in freely admitting I phoned in the rest of my performance as AD (since my lack of authority was made clear to me that day). In hindsight, I should have gotten in my car and driven home—after instructing anyone else on the crew who wanted to do likewise to follow me.[81] Instead, we stuck around and made sure the production wrapped. Sadly, to this day I've never seen a copy of the finished film. I'm not even sure it was finished and released. What a slap in the faces of all of us on that crew who stuck it out to help these inept producers complete shooting. To this day, I am genuinely infuriated by the memory of this project.

Unfortunately, there are worse scenarios than the story I just shared. On February 20, 2014, twenty-seven-year-old camera assistant Sarah Jones lost her life on the set of the film *Midnight*

---

[81] That is correct, I am advocating for mutiny here. In this particular instance, it would most definitely have been the right choice.

Rider, when she was struck by a train. Other crewmembers were injured and maimed. She and others of the crew were standing on a narrow truss bridge for a set of train tracks and had been assured that no more trains would be coming down those tracks that night. However, the producers and director failed to follow protocol for shooting on active train tracks and did not have a representative from the railroad company on site. The producers and director faced manslaughter charges and the Jones family filed a lawsuit against the production company behind the film; claiming that proper permission to be on that property and specifically, on the tracks and bridge, were never secured by the producers. History was made when the film's director, Randall Miller, pleaded guilty to involuntary manslaughter and criminal trespass. He was given two years in prison and eight years of probation, during which he cannot be in charge of a film crew. Before this, no one had ever gone to prison as a result of a death on a film set. In addition to the sentence handed to the director, the assistant director of the film, Hillary Schwartz, was found guilty of criminal trespass and involuntary manslaughter. She was sentenced to 10 years probation, which includes a ban on her ability to work as a producer, director, assistant director, or any other job on a film set that might involve overseeing the safety of the cast and crew. If you ask me, they all got off easy. A young woman is dead. I know I am not alone when I say that I hope that the *Midnight Rider* case serves as a wakeup call to all filmmakers that safety matters and the lives of each individual member of the cast and crew is irreplaceable.

For anyone who has been on film sets, we know that this was a completely avoidable situation. Safety considerations should have pushed producers to search for a different location that possibly had a long-inactive train track or followed careful protocol to make sure that the tracks would in fact be inactive during their shooting time. As a producer myself, my heart breaks for the Jones family and for all the crewmembers who were injured. Such a tragedy simply would not have happened if the wellbeing of the crew and cast had been truly valued by the producers.[82]

It can be quite tempting for artists to think that somehow the ends justify the means. I have mentioned a couple of examples in this book of far less than ideal projects I have worked on. In these cases I have to say the ends did not justify the means. Even if the feature film producer/director I mentioned in Chapter Four, in the section about shot listing, or those short film producers I described above had succeeded in created a legitimately breathtaking film, I would still have no interest in revisiting our working relationships on further projects. I have seen the feature film I talked about in Chapter Four. It is not an entirely bad film, but it does have some key factors that demonstrate clearly the folly of taking on such an egocentric and uninformed approach to directing and producing a film.[83]

Even setting aside the issues I have talked about already, the mere fact that the producer/director from Chapter Four consistently gave actors line readings as his only instructions is one significant example of his lack of respect for the talent of his cast. He should have been offering them playable direction, which

---

[82] I foresee that with the increasing quality of visual effects, a scene like the one they were attempting to shoot will most safely be done in a studio against a green screen.

[83] The key factors that demonstrate this folly in the case of this feature film are: a thin and incoherent story, haphazard visual storytelling, visual effects that are at times laughably bad, and poorly done ADR that is so distracting it ruins even the moments when the film does manage to offer up some genuine emotions and beautiful visuals.

would have ultimately lead to better performances and would have demonstrated respect for the actors as the skilled partners they should have been in the creation of the film. Even if we offer him the benefit of acknowledging that he lacked experience as a director, I regularly spoke with him about this very issue while shooting and his response consistently was one of indifference, which is only a bigger slap in the face of the cast, as his continued giving of line readings was not out of a lack of awareness, but willful ignorance.[84] As a result, I am not the only person who worked on that production that has cut professional ties with this particular filmmaker. I bring all of this up to drive home a very important point: the ends do not justify the means!

Yes, it can be wonderful to be able to say one was involved in a critically acclaimed project, but I believe in the dignity and value of every person on a film's cast and crew. I've been an intern in Hollywood and I've been a green production assistant on a feature film. At my Hollywood internship, I was treated quite poorly (though ultimately my boss had good things to say to me when my time drew to an end). On the feature film that I was a production assistant for years ago, I was treated with warmth and grace (even when I made mistakes). It was a wonderful experience! I sincerely believe a production can be judged by how the "lowest" crewmembers are treated. I believe building a team around respect and collaboration ultimately lends the greatest and most lasting results.

---

[84] For more information on why giving actors line readings is just plain bad directing, please read *Directing Actors* by Judith Weston, listed in the appendices.

Building a Team

When you really value the people you are working with, you will not see them as mere cogs in some machine that churns out films. They will truly be your team members (and you, theirs). If you show this kind of value for each member of your cast and crew, you will find that enthusiasm for the project will catch like a wildfire. One of the things we make a point of doing on our sets with Stories by the River is to always be sure to take care of people's physical needs, as well as doing all we can to keep production on schedule so people can go home at a decent hour. We feed people well and make sure they have a safe place to be out of the elements. The result is that people we work with find that we run a professional and fun set. These people return time after time to volunteer for the subsequent short film projects we produce. They know that we value them and their well-being! We want them to succeed and grow in their talents and skills. They know that a weekend spent on one of our sets is a weekend of working with many talented people, laughing a lot while doing serious and high quality work, getting several good meals, acquiring more hands-on experience, and receiving another IMDb credit. In addition, I always make it a point to thank everyone because I know I can dream up a story, but I can't make the movie alone.

When you view the people you work with as a team, longevity becomes a real possibility. It isn't just about this project, but also about the many more projects still to come, possibly even a project that one of these team members will go on to produce or write or direct. For this reason, great producers look past the present and carefully consider how choices made for a production today might affect people tomorrow. This doesn't mean that a producer will not inconvenience people, if it is essential to the production, such as a scene that needs to be shot at a remote location or at a late hour. Sometimes such inconveniences are part of the reality of filmmaking. As long as such issues are openly addressed upfront during the hiring and planning process, I see no reason why cast and crew cannot be asked to take on reasonable challenges and inconveniences. After all, not all films can be shot on a soundstage or at your friend's spacious apartment. The point is, a good producer will creatively address these challenges in an open manner with all those involved and find ways to help ensure the cast and crew's well-being is cared for during such challenging shoots.

So remember, whether you are paying your cast and crew or they are volunteering, it is a major commitment (even a sacrifice) to work extremely hard for long hours on a film production. Never take this for granted!

Finding Locations

Think through your shooting day and each location involved. If you are making a very concise short film, you are likely going to be at one location. This simplifies things significantly as moving the whole crew to a new location is always a major drain on time, but sometimes, it cannot be avoided as not all films can be made in one location. It is best to think carefully through how the process of moving to a new location will take place and how much time will realistically be required to pack up all the gear and move to the second location and set up all the gear again. If possible, each location should be scheduled for its own shooting day so you don't have to give up precious shooting time for moving everything to a new location. Of course, this is an ideal scenario. Sometimes your script will call for four or five locations, but you'll only have two or three shooting days.

With each new location, you will want to think through as many of the practical considerations as possible ahead of time. How well do you know the locations you will be shooting? Do you have an understanding of where the power sources are located? Do you know where the breaker box is located? It is easy to plug a few too many high-powered lights into the same circuit and trip a breaker. Suddenly, your set goes dark. It's better to know ahead of time where such things are located rather than lose time on set searching, in the dark, or making phone calls to the location's owner (if they happen to not be present).

What is the parking situation at each location? It can be easy to forget that even a modest crew often represents several vehicles (easily a dozen or more) convening at a location and therefore, parking can become difficult. If you are shooting in a major city, parking can be elusive and expensive. You may have to consider car-pooling to the location to decrease the total number of vehicles that need to find parking, which will need to be organized ahead of time to be accomplished well.

Of course, if you are shooting in any public space or city, you may well need permits to shoot. Even if you are shooting in the country; if you need to be on public property or need to be on a road—possibly even need to temporarily block a road—it is best to go through the proper channels and get the permits needed for such shooting. You can generally find the information necessary to apply for permits by calling your local film office. Every state and most major cities have a film office that handles locations, permits, and other valuable information for film productions, such as tax incentives. Film offices may be mostly concerned with large productions coming into the state, but they often are quite happy to help small, local productions as well. In some cases, you will find that you may need to pay for a permit or pay a state employee to be present during the time your crew is shooting on state property (depending on a given state's rules). You can always gather such information ahead of time and then make an informed decision on whether such a location will fit within your budget or if you need to keep looking for a different location, for example, private property that you can be granted access, for free.

Does your film involve guns and stunts or other potentially alarming elements? You will also want to notify the local police department and be sure they are aware of what you are doing. In 2014, four Massachusetts men were arrested when a passerby witnessed what he thought was an armed robbery taking place in a gas station. He called the police immediately! Unfortunately, the four men were only shooting a scene for an amateur movie. The local police, already on edge due to a shooting incident the week before, took no changes and swarmed the gas station, guns out, and arrested the four men. While the gas station owner had granted permission to the filmmakers to shoot their scene on his property, they were ultimately charged with disorderly conduct due to the alarm they had caused to the community and the police department. The very contrite filmmakers pleaded guilty and were sentenced to community service.[85]

Another consideration is to carefully take note of key characteristics of a location and think through how they will

---

[85] See "Four Massachusetts men arrested while acting out robbery scene at convenience store" by Deboray Hasting, New York Daily News, Wednesday, May 21, 2014. www.nydailynews.com/news/national/mass-men-arrested-acting-robbery-scene-convenience-store-article-1.1800661

ultimately play on camera and in the soundtrack. In other words, if you are going to shoot a scene in a building with big windows that have no blinds, you need to visit that location during the time of day you plan on shooting. What will the light be doing? Keeping in mind that the angle of sunlight is constantly changing as the Earth rotates on its axis, imagine how the light will change during the hours of shooting. Will the light present continuity problems when cutting between a shot taken at noon and a shot taken two hours later? There are wonderful apps for smartphones that allow you to pinpoint your location and can give you a visual reference of the trajectory of the sun through the sky so that you can know what kind of sunlight you will be dealing with at various times of the day. And, of course, you also have to keep an eye on the weather!

I also mentioned how a location will work for the soundtrack. You might be wondering what I mean. The degree of difficulty in recording good audio is an aspect of location scouting (or really, of filmmaking in general) that often gets overlooked by new filmmakers. If you are shooting anything other than a silent film,[86] you will need to record good clean audio during shooting. Again, visit the location during the time of day you plan on shooting. If you are shooting on a weekend, try to visit on a weekend. If a weekday, try to visit then. This will give you the most accurate representation of the noise level you are going to be dealing with. Are there busy streets nearby? Are there lots of

---

[86] What I mean by this is that even a scene without dialogue often requires sound. If you need to capture audio on location at all and don't want to invest hours upon hours recreating every footstep, floor creak, jingle of keys, snap of a jacket button, sigh, clunk of a mug set on a table, so forth, then you will want to capture clean audio while shooting. And in that case, you're not actually shooting a silent film—at least not from a production perspective since you still need a sound recordist and a quiet set.

pedestrians? Is there an airport or train tracks in the area? Failing to takes such things into account can lead to problems when shooting. You might find that you spend too much time waiting for an airplane or train to leave the area so you can get clean audio only to encounter the same situation minutes later. You are then faced with having to choose between two bad options: record noisy and inconsistent audio or fall far behind schedule due to very slow progress as you to wait shoot between airplanes or trains or busses. Even if your location is quiet, your ambient sound will change once the room is filled with your crew. The best solution is to record room tone (generally 60 seconds of silence) on the day of the shoot while the crew is present. You will increase your likelihood to have sound that you can use to cover up any inconsistencies that make it to post-production.

As you scout a location you will want to take note of where and how you can turn off the air-conditioning, heat, refrigerator, and any other such appliance that can buzz or hum and ruin audio. Just remember, bad audio is the number one thing your audience will notice that will instantly ruin their experience of your film, even if they do not consciously understand why they feel your movie is bad or "amateurish."

Finally, when it comes to locations, you will also want to note where the crew and cast will be able to hang out between takes and set-ups. Depending on where you are shooting and what time of year, you will want to make sure that everyone has a comfortable place to be away from the elements. Cast will need a place to change and do make-up, everyone will need restrooms, and you will need a place to set up food, coffee, tea, and snacks. You may even need a designated area for smokers to take a smoke break periodically.

Sometimes a location can be ideal from a visual standpoint, but less than ideal in so many other regards that I cannot in good conscious use it. Other times, there are workarounds. If you have access to facilities quite close to set and not much time will be lost in commuting back and forth, it just might be worth it, but only if the location is perfect for your story. Herein lies the key factor: always ask yourself, "Is this location essential to my story?" Or, "Can I accomplish the same thing in a different, but more easily accessible location?"

Another workaround might simply be to choose to shoot a particular project or specific scene with a bare-bones crew, in guerrilla filmmaking fashion (as long as this is done responsibly and does not involve breaking any laws or causing public disruptions). This was my method when directing "Stop." I was my own cinematographer.[87] The film had only one cast member, Trevor C. Duke, who also produced the film with me. Two friends, Mel Hardy and Raz Cunningham, helped in all other regards of shooting. Because of this, we were able to use a park in the area with low impact. And yet, even in that film, the office scene is actually my office where I sit right now writing this.

My point here is simply that you must always come back to the story you are telling, to help you determine what you need to do, in order to shoot the footage the film needs. Do not let delusions of grandeur blind you to the needs of your cast and crew

---

[87] Being both director and cinematographer is something I do *not* recommend to first-time directors. I had already directed several films and shot several other films for other directors by that point. Because of the nature of the story, I felt confident in my ability to direct from behind the camera. Few scripts I have written lend themselves to this kind of directing. Generally, I like to work with a cinematographer and preserve my ability to carefully focus on directing performance rather than worrying about whether a shot is in focus during each take.

or to the practical considerations of your production. In the above example with "Parallel", I needed to know the schedule of the ferry boats that would take us out to the island and when the latest ferry would leave to take us back to shore (as I knew I wanted to shoot as late in the day as possible for the most dynamic sunshine—which meant I also had an eye on the weather). I also treated my actors and DP to dinner between shooting at the island and shooting at the park. It was a very busy half-day of shooting and I had planned out and scheduled every shot I knew I needed using an app called Shot Lister. Because of this careful plan, we were also able to take advantage of opportunities that presented themselves for new shots that we had not thought of until being there together. In the end, we got far more than we originally planned, and the film is much stronger as a result. Overall, it was a fun day of shooting and everyone walked away smiling and excited to meet up again a month later for principal photography.

Setting Deadlines

Whether or not new filmmakers complete projects in this competitive field is a defining characteristic that separates those with potential for longevity from those who are ultimately just talk. This can be especially challenging with short films since they tend to be weekend and off-hour projects. Because of this, it can be quite easy for a short film project to drag on indefinitely. Thus, it is of crucial importance to set deadlines for yourself so that you can guarantee your short film does not stall out and end up abandoned.

In my experience, post-production is where most short films

really tend to stall. It can be exciting to plan out and shoot a short film, but editing can be tremendously tedious and challenging work. Unexpected problems may arise that eat up valuable time in post. Enthusiasm also wanes as it can be easier to feel like working on a new idea instead of completing a project—especially if problems have come to light in editing. For others, perfectionism becomes a very real obstacle. It can be tempting to keep polishing the edit, to keep improving the VFX, to experiment with just one more sound effect or music cue.

If you find you are having troubles with perfectionism keep this thought in mind: perfectionism that paralyzes progress may seem like dedication to the craft, but really it is the manifestation of crippling insecurities. Do not let some unachievable ideal of perfection stand in the way of completing your project! A completed short film that is good or even just okay is far better than a short film that is ever on its way to being perfect, but remains unfinished. At some point, every filmmaker has to say, "good enough", and release their work. I don't mean that you should not have high standards. As I have already indicated in previous chapters, having high standards is essential, but, along with high standards, filmmakers must also have the drive to complete projects in a timely manner.

Many unforeseen things can bring a project to a halt and, while there can be many legitimate reasons for why a short film stalls—as far as the rest of the world is concerned—a project that is abandoned in post-production is no different than a short film that was never shot in the first place. It simply does not exist. A film that remains uncompleted cannot be submitted to festivals or uploaded to YouTube. No one will ever see it. Therefore, I find it is incredibly valuable to set deadlines for projects and communicate those deadlines to all involved from the very beginning. As a matter of fact, this is a core reason why Stories by the River has been able to produce so many short films in such a short time—and I take no credit for this. My fellow producer at SbtR, Kristina Stone Kaiser, has a sharp mind for organizing and planning. From the beginning of pre-production for our first short film, she made sure we had a schedule in mind with deadlines or milestones for various aspects of the project so that the film could be completed and released in a timely manner. This has made all the difference!

Now before you dismiss this talk of deadlines as too rigid, I feel it is important for me to point out that deadlines are still flexible. You should not ignore them, but of course you should also be flexible if and when you encounter legitimate reasons to delay the completion of your film. It is important to be truly honest with yourself, however, about what does and does not constitute a legitimate reason for delaying. Remember how having a shot list does not mean you cannot make changes and adjustments on set? In the same way, having deadlines does not mean you cannot later revise your plan and set new deadlines. Just make sure that you do, in fact, set new deadlines. It can be discouraging to miss a deadline and it can be tempting to move on without setting new ones. Before you know it, a whole year has gone by and people are asking you when they can see the finished film (or worse, they stopped asking you because they assume you've given up and will never finish the movie).

As you start out, you may not have a good sense of how long some aspects of the filmmaking process will take. If you feel unsure of how best to set deadlines (or goals), I encourage you to reach out to other filmmakers either in person or through social media. Ask for advice. Explain what your project entails and be honest about your level of experience. I am positive that you will find many people willing to give you an idea of how long they tend to allow for various aspects of the filmmaking process. As you gain experience, you will be able to identify which areas tend to go smoothly for you and which tend to have snags. With each new project, your deadlines might look quite different as you learn and grow, and as you take on projects with different scopes and requirements. With Stories by the River, we have always evaluated how the process of making each short film has gone as we complete shooting and then, complete post-production. This process of constant evaluation helps us identify what areas need improvement on the next project and whether or not the deadlines we have set are unrealistically quick or too relaxed. In this way, we are able to set new goals for the next project and ensure that specific milestones are reached at appropriate times in order for the next film to be completed in a timely manner.

For Stories by the River projects, we tend to begin with the default goal of having a picture lock (the point where the visual editing is done and timing will no longer change) six weeks after shooting wraps. Our deadlines can be adjusted depending on the length of a given project and other special considerations that may be involved in editing a given short film. If a project is rather straightforward, we'll allow for another four to six weeks for color correction, music composition, and sound mixing. For projects with a lot of VFX, we have allowed a lot more time, but having deadlines for the picture lock and final delivery helps us to keep projects moving forward.

The most important deadline is the delivery date. This is the day you either deliver your completed film to a distributor, begin festival submissions, or you release the film online. If you really want to give yourself motivation to complete your short film, announce publicly when you will be releasing or completing the film. Go ahead and do this even while the film is still in post. Now that date is out there and people know about it. Talk about motivation! Plus, this is a great way to begin building some excitement and buzz about your project before it comes out.

As you go about setting goals and deadlines for your projects, keep in mind that the point of setting deadlines is to help keep you motivated and on track. It is not a means to make yourself a slave to your projects or a reason to throw quality out the window in an effort to crank out a project as quickly as possible. You will need to experiment and discover for yourself what kinds of deadlines are realistic and most helpful for you and the projects you are making. However you go about setting deadlines, the important thing is that you go into each new short film project with at least a rough timeline, with deadlines for when various aspects of the project will be completed. This way, you can be sure that your film will be finished and not become just another one of the many short films that were started, but ultimately abandoned somewhere along the way.

Closing Thoughts

My advice to filmmakers should be clear by now: embrace planning and embrace change. It can be so tempting to just run out and try to shoot. After all, in many ways, that's the fun part. Certainly nothing will teach you how to be a filmmaker quite as well as actually just getting out there and shooting but, with a little investment in pre-production, the shooting and editing experience can be that much more pleasurable and yield greater results.

My hope is that you will embrace the challenges of short filmmaking in this new age of digital media. Discover the stories that move you and, in the process, you will likely uncover stories that might just move many. You might also forge lasting relationships with the people you work with on film after film. In the end, such relationships may far outlast any particular project and bring much greater joy than you ever anticipated. It sure has for me!

The tools for excellent filmmaking at even the smallest budget now exist. A free YouTube, Vimeo, Facebook, or Twitter account can give you access to a global audience, if you can manage to grab enough people's attention. It will be the honing of the skills required to make good films, the depth of your own exploration of life's big questions as you seek to tell worthwhile stories, and your value of each person you work with that will ultimately set you apart. And by this, I don't mean these things will guarantee you will make a short film that goes viral. No one can guarantee that, as cultural tastes are always changing. Managing to garner that kind of attention can be ever elusive but, by embracing such a focus and value system, you will be able to make films you are proud of, with people you love. Even if your films never go viral or win big festival awards, they are stories that do manage to impact the audiences that do see them.

I hope you will get busy with your own ideas and create something beautiful, challenging, haunting, thrilling, or moving. Who knows where it could go... and maybe our paths will cross out there in the digital realm or beyond. In the mean time, I want to invite you to check out the exclusive webpage I have created for this book. It contains additional content, short screenplays you can download, videos, and more. To access this exclusive bonus material, go to: www.mikelwisler.com/#!sf20/dzzl7. Be sure to enter the password: SF2.0@2016.

Now, let's go create!

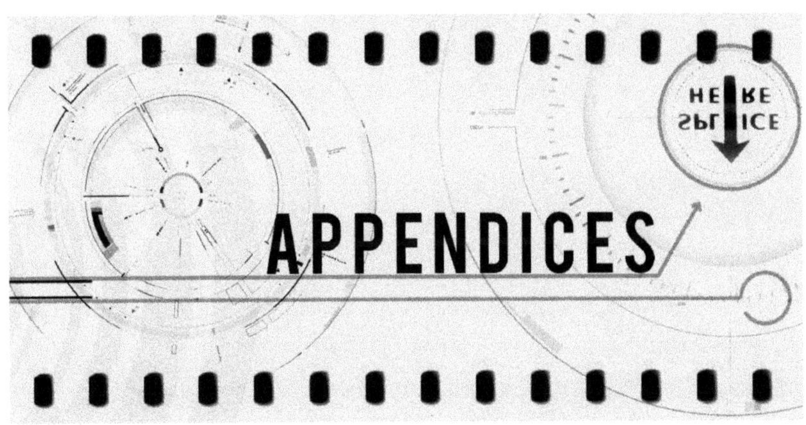
APPENDICES

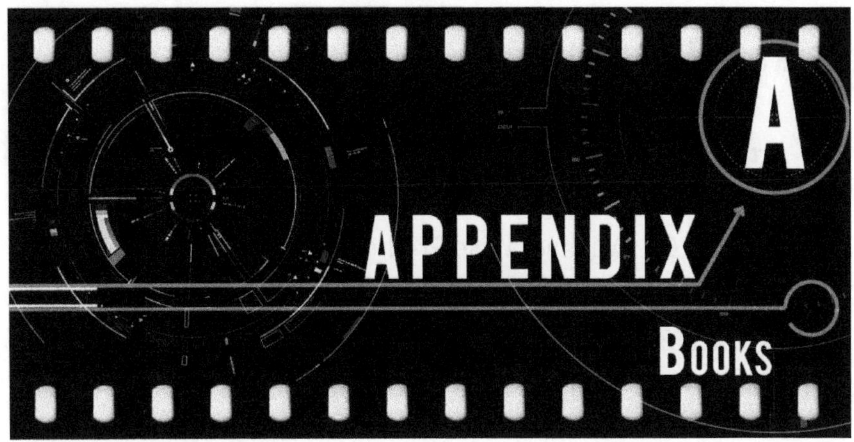

Books on Directing:

Directing 101 by Ernest Pontiff
(Studio City, CA: Michael Wise Productions, 1999)

Direct Actors: Creating Memorable Performances for Film and Television by Judith Weston
(Studio City, CA: Michael Wise Productions, 1996)

Directing: Film Techniques and Aesthetics by Michael Rabiger
(Newton, MA: Focal Press, 1997)

Film Directing Shot by Shot by Stephen D. Katz
(Studio City, CA: Michael Wise Productions, 1991)

The Film Director's Intuition: Script Analysis and Rehearsal Techniques by Judith Weston
(Studio City, CA: Michael Wise Productions, 2003)

Making Movies by Sidney Lumen
(New York, NY: Vintage Books, 1996)

Books on Producing:

The Art of Film Funding: Alternative Financing Concepts by Carole Lee Dean
(Studio City, CA: Michael Wise Productions, 2007)

Film & Video Budgets by Deke Simon and Michael Wiese
(Studio City, CA: Michael Wise Productions, 2001)

Independent Feature Film Production: A Complete Guide From Concept Through Distribution by Gregory Goodell.
(New York, NY: St. Martin's Griffin, 1998)

The Reel Truth: Everything You Didn't Know You Need to Know About Making an Independent Film by Reed Martin
(New York, NY: Faber and Faber, Inc., 2009)

This Business of Film: A Practical Guide to Achieving Success in the Film Industry by Stephen R. Greenwald and Paula Landry
(New York, NY: Lone Eagle, 2009)

Books on Filmmaking (technical):

Cinematography Theory and Practice: Image Making for Cinematographers, Directors, and Videographers by Blair Brown
(Burlington, MA: Focal Press, 2002)

The Filmmaker's Handbook: A complete Guide for the Digital Age by Steven Ascher and Edward Pincus
(New York, NY: PLUME, 2013)

Master Shots by Christopher Kenworthy
(Studio City, CA: Michael Wise Productions, 2012)

Books on Writing:

Bird by Bird: Some Instructions of Writing and Life by Anne Lamott
(New York, NY: Archer Books, 1995)

Lew Hunter's Screenwriting 434: The Industry's Premier Teacher Reveals the Secrets of the Successful Screenplay by Lew Hunter
(New York, NY: Perigee Books, 1993)

The Plot Thickens: 8 Ways to Bring Fiction to Life by Noah Lukeman
(New York, NY: St. Martin's Press, 2002)

The Screenwriter's Problem Solver: How to Recognize, Identify, and Define Screenwriting Problems by Syd Field
(New York, NY: Dell Trade Paperback, 1998)

Story by Robert McKee
(New York, NY: Harper Entertainment, 1997)

On Writing by Stephen King
(New York, NY: Scribner, 2000)

Wired for Story: The Writer's Guide to Using Brain Science to Hook Readers from the Very First Sentence by Lisa Cron
(Berkley, CA: Ten Speed Press, 2012)

Writing Short Films: Structure and Content for Screenwriters by Linda J. Cowgill
(New York, NY: Lone Eagle, 2005)

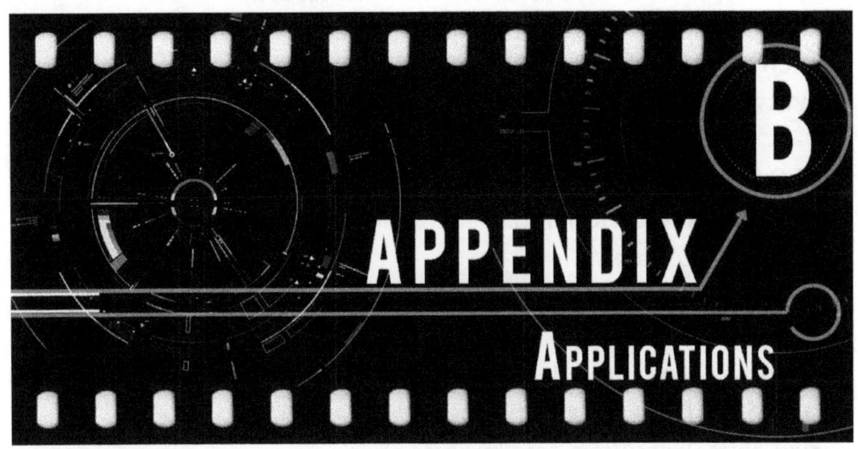

Ardour for MacOS and Linux
Open source multi channel audio recording and mixing app.
(www.ardour.org)

Blender for Windows, MacOS, and Linux
Open source VFX and motion graphics app.
(www.blender.org)

Celtx for Windows, MacOS, iOS
Writing, scheduling, budgeting, and reports.
(www.celtx.com)

DaVinci Resolve Lite for Windows and MacOS
Free editing and color grading app.
(www.blackmagicdesign.com/products/davinciresolve)

Final Draft for Windows, MacOS, iOS
Screenwriting.
(www.finaldraft.com)

Lightworks for Windows, MacOS, and Linux – open source video editing app.
(www.lwks.com)

Movie Magic Screenwriter for Windows and MacOS

Screenwriting.
(www.write-bros.com)

MPEG Streamclip for Windows and MacOS
Free video conversion app.
(www.squared5.com)

Preference Manager for Windows and MacOS
Back-up, restore, and deleted preference files for FCP X, Premiere Pro, Avid, After Effects, and more.
(www.digitalrebellion.com/prefman)

Script Speaker (web-based)
Upload a script, cast it, and listen to it.
(www.scriptspeaker.com)

Shot Lister for iOS, Android, Windows, and MacOS
Scheduling and shoot administration.
(www.shotlister.com)

Story by Adobe (web-based)
Screenwriting and writing collaboration.
(www.adobe.com/story)

Video Space Calculator for MacOS, iOS, and web-based
Calculate the required storage space for your projects depending on type of footage you will be shooting.
(www.digitalrebellion.com/webapps/video_calc.html)

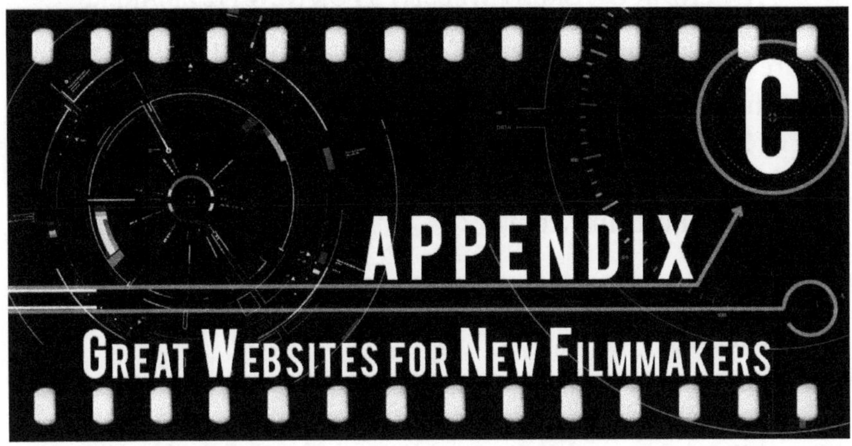

Cinema 5D – digital filmmaking news and equipment reviews.
(www.cinema5d.com)

DSLR Film Noob – podcasts on everything new filmmakers need to know.
(www.dslrfilmnoob.com)

Film Festival Secrets – great guide to getting your films into festivals.
(www.filmfestivalsecrets.com)

Film Freeway – film festival submission website (with many free festivals).
(www.filmfreeway.com)

Film Riot – video tutorials, interviews, and competitions for new filmmakers.
(www.filmriot.com)

Films Short – extensive library of short films.
(www.filmsshort.com)

Frugal Filmmakers – tips and reviews for inexpensive filmmaking.
(www.frugalfilmmakers.com)

Future Shorts – extensive collection of excellent short films. (www.futureshorts.com)

I Love Short Films – watch, share, and read about short films. (www.iloveshortfilms.com)

Indiewire – an online resource and community for independent filmmakers.
(www.indiewire.com)

Micro Filmmaker – an online publication for low-budget filmmakers.
(www.microfilmmaker.com)

No Film School – how-to articles and reviews about digital filmmaking.
(www.nofilmschool.com)

Phillip Bloom – cinematographer and director who reviews nearly every new camera on the market.
(www.philipbloom.net)

Short Film of the Week – watch the best short films online. (www.shortoftheweek.com)

American Cinematographer – interviews with the cinematographers for the biggest films in theaters. Highly technical but incredibly enlightening.
(http://www.theasc.com)

Digital Video – articles and reviews of gear and software and a look inside the production and post-productions of indie and Hollywood films.
(www.digitalvideomagazine.com)

Filmmaker Magazine – focused on independent film, offering articles, links, and resources.
(www.filmmakermagazine.com)

HDVideoPro – covering HD production gear and techniques for TV and film.
(www.hdvideopro.com)

Indie Slate – covering news in the independent film industry.
(www.indieslate.com)

Mix – professional audio and music production.
(www.mixonline.com)

MovieMaker Magazine – covering directing, acting, cinematography, and independent film news.

(www.moviemaker.com)

Pro Audio Review – covering audio gear and techniques for production sound recording and music production.
(www.prosoundnetwork.com)

Pro Moviemaker – covering production gear and techniques for video and film.
(www.promoviemaker.net)

Video Edge – covering latest technology for video and film productions.
(www.videoedge.net)

Videography – covering latest technology for video and film productions.
(www.creativeplanetnetwork.com)

Videomaker Magazine – covering latest technology for video and film productions.
(www.videomaker.com/magazine)

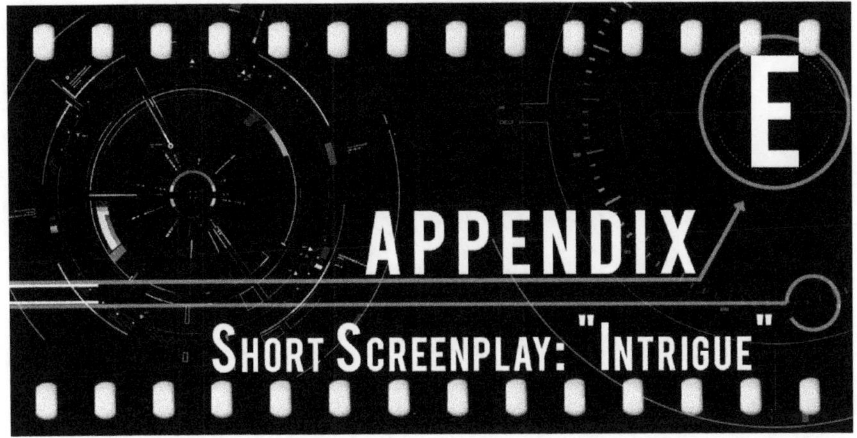

"Intrigue" is a short film I wrote and directed for Stories by the River in 2015. The script idea began when an intriguing visual popped into my mind: a gun taped under a table. From there, this scenario took shape and I quickly wrote the script.

I have included the screenplay here as an example of a single location short film script with only two characters. It's incredibly simple, and yet our team at SbtR seized the opportunity to create a visually engaging film and tell a funny story. I credit the cast, Diana Porter and Aaron Andrade, for fully immersing themselves in the characters and making this ridiculous idea both believable and hilarious.

You can see the finished short film for free by going to www.storiesbytheriver.org. By looking at both the film and script you will be able to compare how the cast made the lines their own and how the film varies from the script in places, due to location, blocking, shot choices, and so forth. We also used a very distinct approach in the visual grammar for the first half of the film and a different visual style for the second half due to the abrupt change that occurs in the middle of the script.

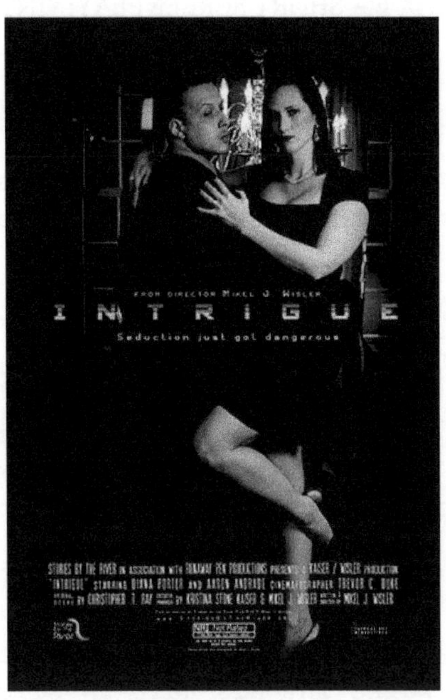

INTRIGUE

written by

Mikel J. Wisler

Short film produced by
Stories by the River
In association with
Runaway Pen Productions.

DOWNLOAD A DIGITAL COPY OF THE "INTRIGUE" SCRIPT BY GOING TO:
WWW.MIKELWISLER.COM/#!SF20/DZZL7
(enter password: SF2.0@2016).

APPENDIX E – SHORT SCREENPLAY: "INTRIGUE"

FADE IN:

CLOSE-UP: A HANDGUN is taped to the underside of a table. A woman's hand runs over it, ensuring the tape is secure.

INT. DINING ROOM - NIGHT

NATASHA (30s) sits at the table. On it sits a bottle of whisky and two glasses. She stands, walking to the window. Cautiously, she peeks through the blinds. She wears a sleek black dress. Her hair and make-up are spectacular.

She moves back into the dining room. Just then, ANTONIO (30s) walks in. His hair is slicked back, he's clean-shaven, and he wears slacks, a dress shirt, and tie.

NATASHA
Welcome, Antonio. I see you have found the place.

ANTONIO
It is not my custom to meet in such an unfamiliar place. But for you, Natasha, I will make an exception this one time.

Her eyes narrow and she grins.

NATASHA
Would you like something to drink?

ANTONIO
Yes. That would be fine.

Natasha pours him a glass and offers it to him.

Antonio takes it, but doesn't drink. She watches him.

NATASHA
Are you not going to drink?

ANTONIO
I never drink alone.

Her eyebrows rise. She pours a glass for herself.

Maintaining distrustful eye contact, they both take a sip. Both purse their lips and frown at the bite of the alcohol.

NATASHA
Please, have a seat.

She indicates the end of the table opposite from the one where she hid the gun.

Antonio complies.

As Natasha takes a seat, Antonio checks her out.

Natasha looks up, catching him. His eyes dart up to hers.

She smiles, in control.

NATASHA (CONT'D)
Do you have the diamonds?

ANTONIO
Let's just say they're in a secure place.

NATASHA
The agreement was that you would have the diamonds and I would give you the nano... bots...

ANTONIO
The Nanorobotic Weapon. Yes. The perfect killer. Invisible, silent, and completely programmable.

He smiles now, confident.

NATASHA
Yes. Those.

She reaches into the front of her dress and retrieves a small vial from her bra.

She sets it down on the table.

NATASHA (CONT'D)
Now, the diamonds.

ANTONIO
My dear Natasha, I said I have them in a safe place.

Natasha SLAMS her hand down on the table hard!

UNDER THE TABLE: The GUN SHAKES, the masking tape loosening.

NATASHA
THAT WAS NOT THE DEAL!

ANTONIO
How do I know you aren't just giving me an empty vial?

Natasha looks down at the vial, a flash of uncertainty.

NATASHA
You will just have to trust me.

ANTONIO
And if I don't trust you?

NATASHA
It does not matter. You did not bring my diamonds.

ANTONIO
I assure you I can retrieve them.

NATASHA
You will do no such thing. I cannot let you leave here.

ANTONIO
Then how do you expect to get your diamond?

Natasha stands up, turning her back to him.

Antonio blinks, surprised. His eyes dart between the vial on the table and Natasha.

NATASHA
I tired of your games, Antonio.

She whirls around.

NATASHA (CONT'D)
WHERE ARE MY DIAMONDS!

She SLAMS both hands down on the table on "diamond."

UNDER THE TABLE: The tape gives way and the gun DROPS.

The gun hits the floor and FIRES!

Natasha and Antonio stand perfectly still, both completely white with terror.

Slowly, Antonio looks down at his body, then back to the wall behind him.

On the wall is a BULLET HOLE.

Antonio slowly looks back up to Natasha, shaken.

ANTONIO
Susan, what the hell?

NATASHA
Are you okay?

ANTONIO
Yeah, but the wall's not!
What was that?

NATASHA
I taped your gun under the
table so I could pull it out
at the right time and subdue
you.

ANTONIO
Why didn't you unload it first?!

NATASHA
Who keeps a loaded gun in the house, Jeff?!

Natasha, well, actually Susan, throws her hands up.

Antonio, or uh... Jeff, stands up.

JEFF
Of course I keep it loaded. If someone breaks in, I'm not going to have time to load the stupid thing, am I?!

SUSAN
WHAT IF ONE OF THE KIDS FOUND THE GUN?!

This stops Jeff cold. His mouth drops open.

JEFF
Well... it's not like they know where it is or anything.

Susan puts her hands on her hips and glares at Jeff.

SUSAN
I have caught Aaron twice snooping around our bedroom closet. And Katy would love to give Aaron a good scare to get him back for what he did last Halloween! And you keep a LOADED WEAPON IN THE HOUSE?!

JEFF
Well, I'm just trying to keep everyone safe!

SUSAN
Oh well, fantastic job!

Jeff stomps over to her and points his finger in her face.

JEFF
You're one to talk. A real gun is not a toy! You practically shot me!

SUSAN
It would've served you right!

JEFF
Oh great, that's just what you'd want, huh? I bet you wish you would have shot me.

SUSAN
If it would shut you up.

He clenches his fists at his side in rage and stares at her.

She glares back.

Finally he throws his hands up.

JEFF
Well, that kind of ruins the evening. Waste of our baby sitter budget. And now I have a whole in the wall to repair.

SUSAN
Well, you have two hours before the kids are home.

Jeff huffs.

JEFF
Hardware store's not open now.

They look off in different directions.

JEFF (CONT'D)
I can't believe you almost shot me.

SUSAN
I can't believe you keep a loaded gun in the house. Way to ruin sex night!

They stand there for a long moment, staring off in anger.

SUSAN (CONT'D)
Well... we did pay for three hours of babysitting.

Jeff just grunts.

SUSAN (CONT'D)
You're such an idiot!
(beat)
Wanna go have angry sex?

Jeff turns and glares at her. Beat.

JEFF
Yeah...

They walk out of the dining room.

CLOSE-UP: The hole on the wall.

FADE OUT.

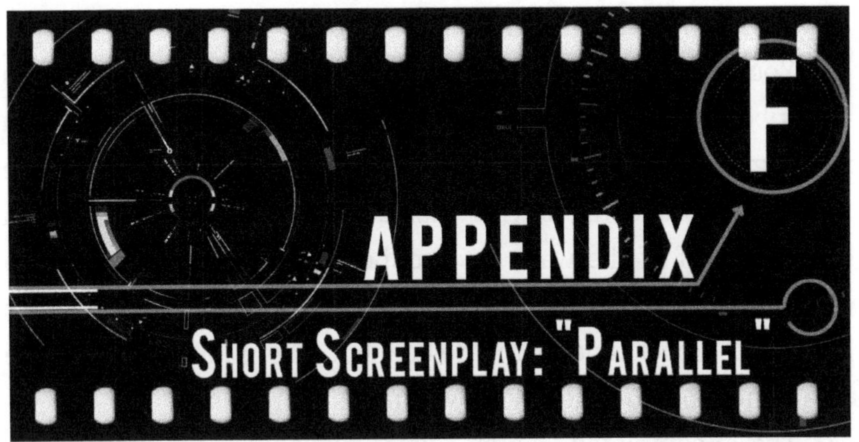

I wrote and directed "Parallel" for Stories by the River in 2014. In Chapter Four, I detailed how the story for "Parallel" took shape, which may be worth revisiting before reading the script. I include the script for "Parallel" here as an example of a much more ambitious short film production compared to "Intrigue" because of the high concept, the number of characters and locations involved, the length of production, and the careful planning due to VFX and production design considerations. It also serves as an example of how much story can be covered in eleven pages by hinting at backstory while focusing on moving the plot forward.

I must give a lot of credit to my cast. Juan C. Rodríguez and Kate Paulsen manage to convincingly take us on a journey of falling in love and facing heartbreak in such a short timeframe. This was such an emotionally charged story and it was thrilling to see it come to life. One of my favorite memories is of the final day of principal photography while we shot the scenes between Paul Kandarian (Henry at the end of his life) and Erica Derrickson (Henry's daughter). After calling cut on one of the takes where Paul, as Henry, has poured out his heart to his daughter, I looked over at our makeup artist, Maya Landi, who stood there off camera wiping tears from her eyes.

You may notice subtle changes in the production design as described in the script compared to what we actually utilized in filming. As production drew closer, a few factors played into the decision to take the device that serves as a window between universes off of the wall, as described in the screenplay, and to place it on a table that would allow not only our actors access around the back side of the device, but also allowed us to place the camera behind the device with much more ease.

The completed film is available for free at www.storiesbytheriver.org. It has been honored with a 2015 PS Award from Rogue Cinema (www.roguecinema.com) as well as being nominated for Best Visual Effects at the 2015 Maverick Movie Awards. It has also won the Best Short Film category at the 2016 Philadelphia Independent Film Awards and has enjoyed quite a positive reception from film critics.

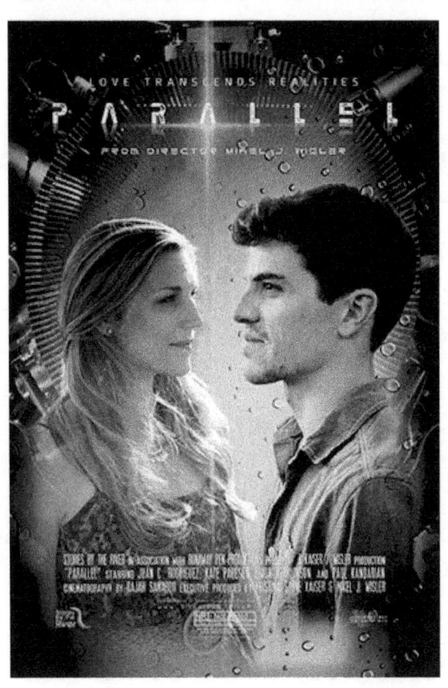

PARALLEL

written by

Mikel J. Wisler

Short film produced by
Stories by the River
In association with
Runaway Pen Productions.

SHOOTING SCRIPT

DOWNLOAD A DIGITAL COPY OF THE "PARALLEL" SCRIPT BY GOING TO:
WWW.MIKELWISLER.COM/#!SF20/DZZL7
(enter password: SF2.0@2016).

ECU MACRO: BUBBLES IN A CLEAR LIQUID.

WOMAN (V.O.)
What is it, dad? What did you want to tell me?

OLD MAN (V.O.)
I... I was there... when the world changed.

INT. BEDROOM - DAY

A glass with SODA WATER sits on a night stand. Next to it, a HOLOGRAPHIC SCREEN hovers in the air displaying VITALS.

HENRY (70s) lies in his bed. Sitting on the bed next to him, VERONICA (30s) looks at her father with concern.

VERONICA
You mean, your research?

Henry coughs, shaking his head.

HENRY
There's something I never told you about my work.... I'm sorry, honey. How are things with Eric?

Veronica shrugs.

VERONICA
The same. Don't really want to talk about it.

Henry nods. He looks off, flooded with memories and emotions fighting for some means to be formulated into words.

VERONICA (CONT'D)
What is it, dad?

HENRY
When I was your age, I was working in Geneva on the Everett Project.

EXT. GENEVA, SWITZERLAND - MAGIC HOUR

TIME LAPSE: Shots of buildings in Geneva (2nd Unit).

INT. RESEARCH FACILITY - DAY

YOUNGER HENRY (30s) stands before a MARKER BOARD, complex equations scrawled out over its surface. TARA (30s) stands next to him. They stare at the board and talk, though we can't hear them.

The small room has COMPUTERS AND MONITORS. Against one wall stands a large ROUND GLASS FRAME with several large CABLES running out of it into the computers.

HENRY (V.O.)
The project was small, underfunded. No one believed it would work. But it was the perfect time for our work. CERN's particle accelerator had proven the existence of the Higgs boson, that most elementary particle.

The Tara points at one particular part of the equation.

HENRY (V.O.)
We were on the cusp of peeling back the veil on

reality itself. By accident we stumbled onto a theory that could finally prove the existence of other universes.

MONTAGE:

1. Younger Henry punches commands into his KEYBOARD.

2. Tara stares at a complex GRAPH on a SCREEN.

HENRY (V.O.)
We were about to open a window into another universe.

3. Younger Henry and Tara stand before the ROUND FRAMED PANE OF GLASS. Tara activates something on a TABLET. The glass in the Frame FLICKERS and FLASHES.

4. Younger Henry and Tara stare at the WHITE BOARD again. Henry circles a section of the equation in red marker.

HENRY (V.O.)
Months of trial and error.

5. Younger Henry sits alone in the darkened room, staring at the FRAME, thinking. He sits forward suddenly.

HENRY (V.O.)
It finally occurred to me that a window of this type has to be opened from both sides.

6. Younger Henry works frantically on a COMPUTER.

HENRY (V.O.)
If there really is an infinite number of other universes out there...

somewhere, someone in at
least one of those universes
might be trying to open a
window too.

7. Tara and Younger Henry stare at the white board again. Henry steps forward and writes beneath the equation: "Multiple Frequencies at one."

HENRY (V.O.)
So we adjusted our approach.

END MONTAGE.

INT. BEDROOM - DAY

Veronica nods.

VERONICA
And that's how you made
contact?

HENRY
Took almost a year of
waiting.

INT. APARTMENT BEDROOM - NIGHT

Younger Henry wakes suddenly as an ALARM CHIRPS on his TABLET. He reaches for it.

The screen shows, "Possible Contact Detected."

He sits up straight.

INT. RESEARCH FACILITY - NIGHT

Younger Henry bursts through the door, followed by Tara. They both stop, starring at--

The Frame GLOWS with life. On the other side, TWO PEOPLE stand, staring back. One is ANNE (30s). Her partner is a Joseph (20s).

HENRY (V.O.)
But we made contact!

Henry steps forward slowly, in awe.

In the Frame, Ann does so as well.

YOUNGER HENRY
Hi.

ANN
(through crackles)
Hi.

The IMAGE in the FRAME FLICKERS. Ann smiles.

INT. BEDROOM - DAY

Henry stares off, a slight smile on his lips.

HENRY
That's when I first saw her. Maybe at first it was the awe of contacting another universe, but ... no, there was always more.

Veronica frowns then slowly understanding washes over her.

VERONICA
You loved her.

HENRY
From that very moment.

INT. RESEARCH FACILITY - DAY

MONTAGE:

1. Younger Henry has the white board closer to the Frame. He talks excitedly about the equation.

HENRY (V.O.)
After the initial fuss, we could finally talk to the other universe. And we did talk. A lot. Ann and I.

2. He sits and EATS talking to Ann through the Frame.

3. On a LAPTOP he shows PICTURES of our history.

4. Ann holds up a TABLET with a NEWS ARTICLE: Elena McCarthy Wins Close Election to Become First Female President.

END MONTAGE.

INT. BEDROOM - DAY

Veronica listens now with intent eyes focused on her father.

VERONICA
You spent a lot of time with her?

Henry grins.

HENRY
Every moment I could spare.

INT. RESEARCH FACILITY - DAY

Ann stands on the other side of the Frame.

Ann reaches out and touches the glass on her side.

Henry reaches out and places his hand opposite of hers against the glass on our side.

HENRY (V.O.)
In all the time we worked to reach this point, I never once imagined I would want anything more that to just ... make contact.

Ann stares longingly through the window.

HENRY (V.O.)
I never thought that once I made contact all I'd want to do was to find a way to break through that damn window.

ANN
Henry, tell me. If you could, where would you take me?

YOUNGER HENRY
Close your eyes, I'll take you there right now.

CU: Their hands on the WINDOW.

EXT. GEORGE'S ISLAND - IMAGINARY SEQUENCE - DAY

MONTAGE:

1. Younger Henry and Ann walk hand-in-hand on the grassy hills atop the old stone fort.

HENRY (V.O.)
In our minds, we travelled.

2. Ann twirls about beneath the large stone archway.

3. Sitting on a rocky cliff, they look out at a Lighthouse.

4. Standing above the fort, they slowly draw close.

HENRY (V.O.)
We touched.

5. Their lips meet slowly.

HENRY (V.O.)
We were together.

[Note: if I shoot this, above montage is only a basic guide. I'll want to improvise much of these moments.]

INT. RESEARCH FACILITY - DAY

6. Henry plugs in an iPod into his computer, gesturing excitedly for Ann to wait. He hits play, and MUSIC SWELLS.

EXT. GEORGE'S ISLAND - IMAGINARY SEQUENCE - DAY

7. In the large field in the center of the Fort, they lay next to each other on the grass, looking up.

HENRY (V.O.)
We found love that reached
across an abyss and through
metaphysical barriers.

8. On the cliff, they kiss as water crashes on the rocks.

HENRY (V.O.)
We never touched ...
physically.

INT. RESEARCH FACILITY - DAY

9. Young Henry and Ann stand on their respective sides of the unrelenting quantum divide, their hands to the glass.

HENRY (V.O.)
We were so close, yet separated by an infinity between us.

END MONTAGE.

INT. BEDROOM - DAY

Veronica fights for composure as she listens.

HENRY
We shared our lives. For almost two years.

Henry stares off, lost in thought.

When Veronica speaks she's surprised that in spite of her efforts, her voice cracks with emotion.

VERONICA
What happened?... Dad. What happened?

Henry stirs.

HENRY
About twenty months in, we were going over detailed information on how each of our sides managed to contact the other...

He sighs.

HENRY (CONT'D)
We discovered ... well, in essence, our math didn't match up.

VERONICA
What do you mean?

HENRY
It's like our universes were moving through reality at slightly different speeds. And for this brief window in time...

He lifts his hands, palms down, holding them almost side by side. He moves them so they drift into perfect alignment.

HENRY (CONT'D)
For this tiny moment, our two universes were in perfect alignment. So we could reach out to each other.

INT. RESEARCH FACILITY - DAY

Younger Henry and Tara stand next to each other. Tara talks (though we don't hear his words).

In the Frame stand Ann and Joseph. Ann and Henry look at each other with heavy eyes.

HENRY (V.O.)
We talked through every possibility, but the data was clear. Our two universes were drifting out of synch with. We had only another three months, at most.

INT. RESEARCH FACILITY - LATER

Younger Henry stares at a computer screen. On the desk he has stacks of scribbled notes.

ANN
Henry. Please.

Ann stands in the Frame. The IMAGE has more static and FLASHES and STUTTERS more often.

ANN (CONT'D)
We've been over this.

YOUNGER HENRY
I can't ...

He looks up at her.

YOUNGER HENRY (CONT'D)
I'm not ready to say goodbye.

ANN
We don't have to say goodbye yet. There's still time.

YOUNGER HENRY
FOR WHAT?!

Ann is taken aback.

ANN
To be with me. Just be with me.

Henry looks away. Beat. He nods.

INT. BEDROOM - DAY

Henry shakes his head.

HENRY
I was young and stupid. I should have stopped trying much sooner. We could have had more time together.

INT. RESEARCH FACILITY - DAY

Henry sits on a stool before the Frame. Ann sits on the other side. The image is significantly FUZZY now.

HENRY (V.O.)
We held on as long as we could.

A DIGITAL CLOCK on a computer counts down the seconds, 20, 19, 18...

YOUNGER HENRY
I love you, Ann.

ANN
(through lots of static)
I love you, Henry.

Their hands reach out, touching the screen.

EXT. GEORGE'S ISLAND - IMAGINARY SEQUENCE - DAY

MONTAGE:

1. Ann runs, Henry chasing.

2. They stand on the rock cliff.

3. They kiss.

END MONTAGE.

INT. RESEARCH FACILITY - DAY

The countdown continues... 12, 11, 10...

Ann and Henry stare at each other through the frame. Ann's IMAGE becoming increasingly filled with STATIC.

The countdown... 8, 7, 6...

Ann's IMAGE is ALMOST GONE. But we can just see the tears slipping down her cheeks.

The countdown... 5, 4, 3...

Henry is breathing hard, hand still on the glass.

HENRY

Ann. ANN!

The countdown... 2, 1, 0.

SILENCE. The WINDOW is nothing but STATIC now. Henry still has his hand up to it.

He stands suddenly, kicking back the stool. He lets out a primal anguished cry, his knees buckling, and he slides down to the floor, back against the wall.

HENRY (V.O.)

Just like that... we were out of synch.

INT. BEDROOM - DAY

Tears slip down Veronica's cheek. Her hand comes to her face.

VERONICA

(barely audible)

Oh dad.

Henry's looking off again. He looks back to his daughter.

HENRY

Oh sweetie, I didn't tell you this so you would cry. I've wanted to tell you for years. I just didn't know how. It's like something from another life. It was so long ago. I spent years being bitter. How could I have fallen in love like that, found someone so amazing... only to lose her? I'm not sure why it happened. I was so angry. But eventually I realized...

He sits up, looking at his daughter.

HENRY (CONT'D)

Not much in this life makes sense. But it seems to me that we're all out of synch. It's like we're all particles flying through the universe at a million miles an hour. And every now and then, we're fortunate enough to discover that for a while our paths run parallel to someone else's. And rather than dread the inevitable moment when our trajectories drift apart, we need to cherish every moment we share.

He shakes his head.

HENRY (CONT'D)

When I finally realized that, I was ready to move on. And a

short while later I met your mother.

He smiles big.

HENRY (CONT'D)
And our trajectories ran side-by-side for years... until I lost her too. But I never regretted a single moment we had together. Even though I thought I could never love like that again, I loved your mother with every bit of my being.

Veronica smiles through tears.

HENRY (CONT'D)
I... just wanted to tell you that. Right now your path runs parallel to other people's paths. No one knows what will happen tomorrow.

Henry coughs.

HENRY (CONT'D)
Never forget this. Don't waste years of your life like I did. Can you promise me that?

Veronica looks intently at her father, tears flowing freely. She's perfectly still. Beat.

CUT TO BLACK.

VERONICA (V.O.)
Okay. I promise.

THE END.

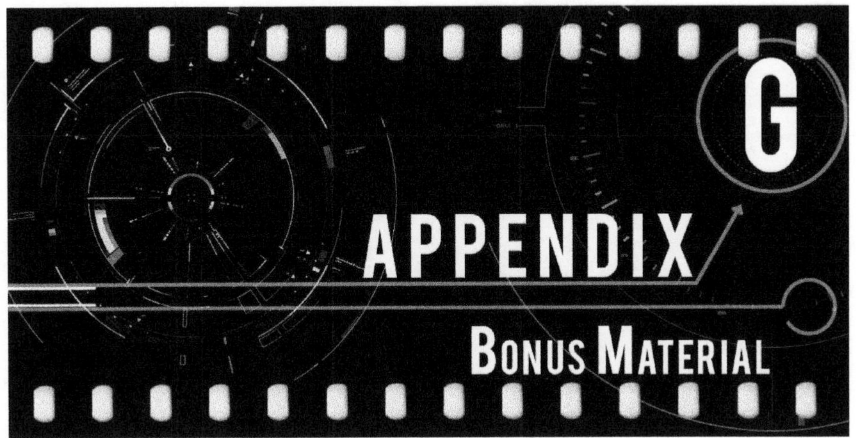

As part of your purchase of this book, I am offering a free downloadable PDF version of two short scripts. To download the scripts visit:

www.mikelwisler.com/#!sf20/dzzl7

(enter password: SF2.0@2016).

The two scripts available for download are "Intrigue" and "Parallel," featured in Appendices E and F. Both films are also available online for free, thanks to Stories by the River. You will be able to access the scripts and the finished film by going to the bonus material link. You will also find additional videos and other materials collected on the Bonus Materials page as well as web-versions of the other appendices, making it easier to quickly access websites listed above.

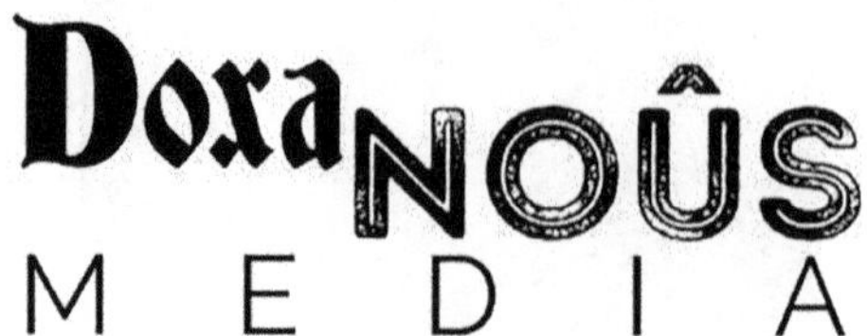

Communicating Belief and Intellect

DOXA: Doxa (from ancient Greek "glory", "praise", "to appear", "to seem", "to think" and "to accept") is a Greek word meaning common belief or popular opinion.
-- A Greek-English Lexicon

NOÛS: Noûs (from Greek philosophy) is a Greek word meaning mind or intellect.
-- Random House Kernerman Webster's College Dictionary

MEDIA:

A substance that makes possible the transfer of energy from one location to another, especially through waves. -- The American Heritage Science Dictionary

---

DoxaNoûs Media is a publishing company focusing on fiction and nonfiction in the areas of entertainment, business, politics, theology, and civil discourse.

facebook.com/DoxaNousMedia | Twitter: @DoxaNousMedia

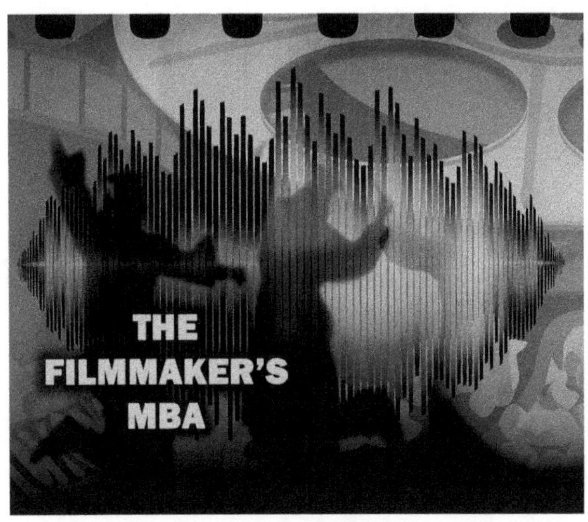
THE
FILMMAKER'S
MBA

MORE BOOKS BY MIKEL J. WISLER

Sleepwalker
Unidentified
Amnesiac (Short story)
Suspicious Behavior
Empathy O.D.

COMING SOON FROM MIKEL J. WISLER

Stop
Ours is a One Way Journey (Short Story)

www.ingramcontent.com/pod-product-compliance
Ingram Content Group UK Ltd.
Pitfield, Milton Keynes, MK11 3LW, UK
UKHW020424250726
13967UKWH00007B/2802

9 781732 530706